Beyond the Shot

Beyond the Shot

INNER WORK FOR LASTING SUCCESS ON WEIGHT-LOSS MEDICATIONS

Jessica Brown

BEYOND THE SHOT
Inner Work for Lasting Success on Weight-Loss Medications
Copyright © 2025 by Jessica Brown

Publisher Information: Inner Well Press
www.innerwellpress.com
ISBN: 979-8-9995037-1-8 (paperback)
      979-8-9995037-2-5 (ebook)

First Edition

Disclaimer: The information in this book is for educational purposes only and is not intended as medical advice. The author and publisher disclaim any liability for any adverse effects arising from the use or application of the information contained in this book. Readers should consult with their healthcare providers before making any changes to their medication regimen or treatment plan.

Trademark Notice: Ozempic® is a registered trademark of Novo Nordisk A/S Wegovy® is a registered trademark of Novo Nordisk A/S Mounjaro® is a registered trademark of Eli Lilly and Company All trademarks are the property of their respective owners.

Cover Design and Typesetting: Geoffrey Bunting
Editor: Lara Asher

www.thelovingdiet.com and www.glp1nutritionacademy.com

For my family, friends, and husband, Derek — my biggest supporters.

For my teacher Dr. Robert Waterman, who taught me that love will have its way and how to put it into practice.

And for my younger parts who prayed for a miracle — that turned out to be me.

Contents

Introduction

My client Emily had endured a lifelong struggle with her body and food that manifested over the years as binge eating at night and dieting during the day. Like many, she had tried "every" diet and constantly cycled through different exercise plans over the years. There were periods when she lost weight, but they were temporary—and only through great effort and deprivation. This left her not only hungry and hopeless but also with a pile of negative beliefs about herself that imprinted every bite of food she ate and every new exercise plan that she thought would finally deliver her into a new place of happiness in her body. Emily believed the inner mental chatter that had played her (untrue) beliefs on continual repeat since childhood. She also believed those (untrue) beliefs would be solved by fixing her mindset or finding the right lifestyle. When she learned the skills to listen closely to her inner mental chatter, she began to understand how it not only prevented her from reaching her goals but also was not true. Endless taunting in childhood and adolescence about the size of her body had, over time, caused her to believe that she was damaged and less than everyone else. That belief snowballed into a cycle of self-punishment in the form of dieting during the day and then revenge and relief by binge eating at night.

Recently, Emily's doctor had diagnosed her with pre-diabetes and suggested she try a GLP-1 medication *(such as Ozempic®, Wegovy®, or Zepbound®).* She was instantly curious but also very hesitant because, after years of being in an endless cycle of punishing her body, she truly believed nothing would work. If there wasn't an element of deprivation, it was just too good to be true. After the first few weeks, she began to lose weight, which she was thrilled about, but more than that, food stopped occupying her thoughts night and day. The nighttime bingeing stopped. Although a whole new set of fears about the GLP-1 medication surfaced with her recent progress, we went to work building her self-compassion skills to reexamine her underlying (untrue) beliefs. This didn't happen with sheer mental strength like she thought it would; it happened through practicing deep compassion toward the part that believed life was punishing her by being in a bigger body. We blended self-compassion exercises with reparenting and parts work, which helped her go back to the early days as a pre-teen when she was constantly bullied, so she could learn how to give that young girl the emotional safety she didn't receive back then. Practicing these skills while the GLP-1 had quieted her food noise resulted in a complete game changer for Emily. She had the time, the space, and the motivation to examine and sort through the very issues she had tried to fix and run away from her whole life. Being on a GLP-1 medication did not heal Emily's untrue beliefs, but it gave her the motivation and a much-needed break from the constant mental chatter, so that she could change them for good and truly have a new relationship with food and her body.

If, like Emily, you're on a GLP-1 medication, you may be feeling hopeful or in control of your health for the first time in a long time. It may feel like the long battle with food and your body is finally over. In my practice I often hear, "Not only did GLP-1 medications change my life—they saved my life." But even if you're thrilled with your journey so far, a small part of you may be wondering "what if I can't be on the medication forever?" or "what if I gain all the weight back?" or even "is this too good to be true?" I assure you it isn't, and this book will show you how to address those fears, as well as others.

The Opportunity We Have Right Now

You're a pioneer in one of the most significant health movements the world has ever seen, and it's just getting started! GLP-1 medications are predicted to be the best-selling medications of our time, outpacing every other drug three times over by the end of 2025. People are increasingly turning to these medications to assist with personal and health goals. Our society is in a state of health-related crisis, and too many are suffering. GLP-1 medications offer numerous benefits, improving various health markers beyond their primary recommendation of Type-2 diabetes. As the FDA expands GLP-1 approval into obesity and heart disease (among many others), the number of users is expected to grow exponentially in the coming years. It's important that everyone receives support and emotional care for the journey. Because, like all pioneers, walking bravely into new territory requires new skills—and this book will teach them to you. Whatever your story and whatever brought you to this book, you truly stand at the forefront of a revolution in healthcare and medicine. As I celebrate this new chapter with you, I'd like to pose a question: Will you take your journey even further?

You have a unique opportunity to address the challenges that brought you here in the first place. A new door has been opened... and it's time to walk *all the way* through it. Now that you're beginning to (finally) feel a newfound peace with food and your body, there is potent, valuable work you can do to make sure it lasts. Beyond the practical nutrition and lifestyle modifications, your journey is beckoning you to go inward, where you can finally transform the relationship you have with food and your body—or any beliefs about being an imposter—without years of therapy. You can do it by learning two simple skills: self-compassion and reparenting.

How you currently see yourself and food is ushering in a new chapter where you can heal the deeper parts within you that still hold misconceptions about your worth, goodness, and value. Finally, there is space without all the food noise. Finally, there are resources. Finally, there is change. I will teach you the inner tools to navigate this new reality and conquer any fears that may still lurk in the corners of your heart. I will help you expand and maintain the positive place you are in today for years to come—because going on a GLP-1 medication is only the beginning. Together, we'll examine what you have believed about yourself... and if it's true. It turns out that matters, especially when you're looking to expand the freedom you've found while on GLP-1 medications. It's something many people skip over, but this inner work will prepare you for the long term physically and mentally, making you stronger, happier, and more at peace.

You may feel closer to your best self than you have in years: hopeful, excited, and energized. Take this opportunity to harness this moment and finally make peace with the hard road that may have brought you here. Doing so will bring a new sense of calm and confidence as you move forward and feel equipped to handle potential future fears. You can heal the parts of you that may feel haunted by the journey that brought you to this moment—despair, bullying, discrimination, hopelessness, shame, loss, powerlessness, and rejection. It's normal to want to put those fears and feelings permanently behind you—and you can with the tools in this book.

I've seen many clients on GLP-1 medications in my clinical and compassion coaching practice in the last two years. I immediately noticed the specific needs they required to navigate the uncharted waters of their journey. Although they have many similarities to others experiencing disordered and emotional eating, those on GLP-1 medications sit in the eye of a cultural hurricane most don't. There is an urgency to make the most of "food noise" being at a minimum. The years of heartache have taken their toll and still linger, even if in the shadows. For as much as GLP-1 is and will be a transformative medication, it's not powerful enough to change all the beliefs and fears you have about your worthiness and goodness—only your heart can do that. And this book will teach you how.

While it's natural to want to close that chapter of a painful past with your body, food, and eating, *it isn't the same as healing it.* Many people worry about the future and fear returning to their old bodies. They want to know a tangible way to sustain the mental and physical healing they are experiencing. But, years of feeling powerless have taken a toll. Hope is often in short supply for those who feel helpless, but GLP-1 medications have brought back hope to millions. You have at your fingertips the ability to learn fundamental skills to heal your past and soothe fears about the future by discovering what root beliefs you may still hold true, even while experiencing the massive benefits of GLP-1 medications. In fact, I'll argue that uncovering these beliefs *while you're on a GLP-1 medication* is truly making the most of your time and energy, even if it may feel daunting. More than healing the belief framework you have been operating out of for years, you can harness an inner healing tool kit, so that this time you can truly have a different relationship with food and your body because you know how to have a different relationship with *yourself.*

Taking a leap of faith with me will change your life. And the approach I'm sharing doesn't focus on healthy eating, willpower, or mindfulness. I'm not going to tell you how to eat, what to think, or how to act. Moreover, you won't have to unlearn or reprogram your mind, and no one will ask you to "fix" your problem or adhere to a specific protocol. Instead, we'll use a tool kit you already have—your heart—to heal your difficult relationship with food and transform your struggle into a teacher who will help you (re)claim your worth, value, and lovability.

This won't always be easy. The biggest transformations that humans experience happen in the heart, followed and supported by the brain— not the other way around. Yet when we allow the heart to tend to our suffering instead of letting the mind fix, correct, and/or solve oursuf- fering, we must take a huge leap of faith in ourselves and force ourselves to feel our pain, trust our pain, and cultivate patience. Fortunately, we all inherently possess the ability to (re)discover our innate goodness and wholeness despite the tragedies of life; I hope today's the day you start leaning into this truth and using it to drive lifelong change.

Many people on GLP-1 medications are receiving a much-needed rest from thinking about food night and day. That's why it's a perfect time to start practicing how to be kind to yourself and unpacking the belief systems you have about your body and food—not judging yourself by your relationship with food—then peace, not happiness, becomes the end point. By learning to identify and soothe the parts of you that believe untruths about yourself, you'll increase your emotional resilience and reduce the need to seek comfort in food. Though you may continue to eat in moments of stress and anxiety, you'll be able to do so without shame-fueled cycles and measurements of self-worth.

This book is my love letter to you. By showing you that it's easier to remember your wholeness than fix what appears to be broken, I'll teach you how to use your heart to heal and to trust yourself through your struggles with food.

What to Expect from Beyond the Shot
The stage is set for change, and I firmly believe that the most fruitful path to get there is one of inward exploration. In this book, I'll help you implement a radically different approach to emotional eating that's catalyzed my own healing and changed the lives of many of my clients. (Please keep in mind that nothing I share in this book is meant to replace medical advice.) On our journey, I'll guide you through exploring life

events and their impact on your belief system. I'll illustrate how what I call "bad data," or the incorrect beliefs we have about ourselves and our self-worth, disrupts our nervous system and influences our present relationship with food and our body. Together, we'll construct a framework for change, utilizing the transformative power of self-compassion and reparenting. By treating yourself as a good friend would treat you (self-compassion) and giving yourself what you did not receive as a child (reparenting), you'll change how you perceive the events of your life, your beliefs, and yourself.

This is the fundamental framework we'll explore:
- What life events have influenced you?
- What (false) beliefs have these life events created?
- How have your beliefs molded your self-perception?
- How do these factors impact your core relationship with food and your body?
- How can self-compassion and reparenting enhance your inner strength and foster self-trust?

By embracing this framework, you'll likely experience:
- Increased emotional resilience for uncertainty in life
- More peace with your body and food
- Enhanced capacity to self-regulate your nervous system
- Self-trust in your ability to handle emotional discomfort
- Reduced dependence on food to compensate for perceived inadequacies

Please know that this book is for beginners and experts alike. If you're a beginner looking for ways to effectively navigate your GLP-1 journey with real emotional tools, this book is definitely for you, whether you are working with a therapist or not. If you're an expert or professional in medicine, nutrition, somatic work, Internal Family Systems, parts work, or alternative cognitive behavioral therapy such as dialectical behavior therapy (DBT) or acceptance and commitment therapy (ACT), looking to help clients in your practice who are on GLP-1 medications, this book is also for you, as it highlights practical tools I've created for emotional eating as well as deeper components of self-compassion, reparenting, and parts work that are not currently taught.

You'll want a journal to take notes, answer questions posed in the chapters, and start building your own care practice after completing the included meditations and exercises. As you go through this book and learn the various exercises, you can discover which combination works best for you to foster inner healing and create lasting change. Throughout, I'll also share my own stories and take you into my practice by sharing sessions with clients. And every chapter ends with concrete takeaways to help you apply what you have learned.

You'll develop practical skills that travel well. Tapping into the power of your heart is something you can practice at will and only requires trust in yourself. Your heart holds the potential to transform your self-perception more effectively than any other person or method. I promise. And more important, scientific research supports this approach.

Let's embark on this journey together toward a life that includes mind, body, and food freedom. Thank you for trusting me to take you there. I look forward to walking with you on the path of self-compassion and reparenting toward a life of inner freedom. It's time to supercharge your GLP-1 experience!

Chapter 1

What Is Your Struggle Story?

Humanity, take a good look at yourself. Inside, you've got heaven and earth and all of creation. You're a world—everything is hidden in you. —Hildegard of Bingen

If you are like many, your transformation with GLP-1 has been everything you could have imagined. You've lost weight, and the benefits have likely been life-changing. And, for many of you, this has come after years of attempting to institute positive lasting change with food and your body. You've been on diets; you've been to therapy; you've done the exercises. So, it may feel like GLP-1 is a magical bypass that has come to fruition. That dark valley you've been traversing, hoping to get to the bridge of transformation, is finally here. It must feel really, really good. So, take a moment to savor it! But those dark valleys you've been walking are journeys that hold valuable information, so we're going to examine them in this chapter to make sure you get the most out of the knowledge they hold. For many of us, remnants from our struggles may still be alive and active, albeit just temporarily out of view while on a GLP-1, and taking the time to examine them is helpful to the overall healing process GLP-1 has started for you. Not only is it helpful, but it's also crucial, so you can build a robust internal support system as you navigate a path forward.

It's essential to acknowledge that a lifetime of challenging experiences and emotions likely forms the backdrop, as you contemplate your life leading up to GLP-1 usage and what your future will hold after you complete your course of medication. In this chapter, we'll explore the personal experiences that create the emotional landscape dictating how you perceive life—what I term the "Struggle Story"—and why examining it holds profound healing potential for the past, present, and future. It's the first step I have my clients take to start addressing fears about the future. You may be hesitant while reading this, but bringing our stories into the open helps us understand the beliefs that form as a result; those beliefs inform your self-perception and decisions concerning your emotional and physical health. Together, let's leverage the mental clarity that GLP-1 medications afford you so that, should you discontinue them, you'll be well-prepared to put your best foot forward for enduring success.

In this chapter, we take full advantage of this shift by delving into your "Struggle Story" and examining the narrative that surfaces as a result. I understand you may want to close the often-painful chapter of the past, but here's why it's important: Our stories are frequently built on untrue beliefs about ourselves, and taking the time to acknowledge and change these untrue "truths" can drastically improve our relationship with food and our bodies moving forward. We'll also discuss our obsession with "fixing" and "rightness," and why they don't ultimately work when it comes to the core relationship we have with food and our bodies, because they ignore that our struggles often contain significant misunderstandings we've created about ourselves that simply aren't true, yet they dictate how we navigate through life. GLP-1 medications are highly effective at building and illuminating space in our hearts and minds, allowing us to unearth our Struggle Stories, acknowledge them, care for them, and heal them. What I'm proposing differs significantly from the thousands of other books written on this subject, because in this book I will show you how to rewrite your Struggle Story to be your Success Story by using your *heart*—not your mind. To do this, we will examine (and then heal) some very important things that impact how you eat, your relationship with food, and how much you like or dislike your body. Closely examining what you believe about yourself and why. We start this process here, at the beginning, by simply writing down your story.

One of My Struggle Stories
I moved to Florida in the third grade. Like most of our neighbors, we had a pool in our backyard. Wearing a swimsuit was almost a year-round

occurrence, which I quickly grew to despise. After my parents' divorce a few years prior, I had sought solace from the pain of missing my mother in food and transformed from a normal-sized kid into a chubby kid. Living in a larger body became a significant issue as I continued to soothe my feelings with food.

Every time I put on a swimsuit at nine, I felt profound unhappiness about my larger body. I can still recall wishing I could wear a bikini instead of the utilitarian one-piece that fit my body better. I remember how much I liked eating and how it became the grounding rod to help me adjust to living in a new state and all the unfamiliar things that came with it. I had a new stepmother (who had suddenly assumed most of my caretaking responsibilities, as my father often traveled for work), home, neighborhood, school, and friends. I also experienced the near-constant heartache of missing my mother, who I only saw twice a year.

After eating an entire Big Mac, I became confused about why I was still hungry. I recall sitting in a McDonald's with my twin sister and stepmother after casually polishing off a Big Mac hamburger, asking myself silently, *How can you possibly still be hungry?* This was one of the initial setups for struggles surrounding my weight.

My Struggle Story from that time was that the deep unhappiness I felt with having a larger body meant life was punishing me by making it ten times harder for me to lose weight than it would be for a naturally thin person. Life back then was dodgy, and for some reason, I deserved the pain I was experiencing. To make sense of my struggle, I made a sweeping decision at nine years old about what life meant: that pain was the new normal, nobody was coming to save me, and food helped my pain. Looking back on that now, I consider it a small miracle that I figured out a coping mechanism for pain at nine years old. Unfortunately for me, I just happened to have genetics that made that route harder because, along with my childhood sorrow, I would be deeply unhappy with my body that couldn't eat everything it wanted and stay slim.

You probably have similar stories, too. We all do. I have an entire list of defining moments in my life that I sometimes reflect on that seemed to indicate I was different, less than, or not as good. As a child, I innocently believed that I had drawn the short straw in the body lottery—a body that would require three times as much work to "look good" compared to everyone else and an internal voice with the sole job of shaming me into executing the willpower required to change it. I have spent years (this is not an exaggeration) doing whatever I could to change my genetic lottery card or hating the universe for giving me the one I had.

There is a strong belief for those of us who work ten times as hard as others to live in a body we like or feel comfortable in that GLP-1 medications will prove to be the answer to our prayers. They may. They certainly provide a much-needed break from the constant self-blame triangle I see my clients caught in. But these medications will not remove the beliefs established due to your Struggle Story. Only you can do that. However, *you can do it,* and after bearing witness to hundreds of clients, it's not as daunting as you might think.

Going back to my story, you may not be surprised to read that I promptly put myself on my first diet at nine years old and lost 10 pounds. *See, Jessica? You can do this. You just have to try harder, be more focused, and learn the tricks of the trade required to be in a body that naturally wants to be fat. You got yourself into this by eating Big Macs—you can get yourself out of it.* I think it's wild that humans use their inner voice as a tool of suffering (hoping for positive change) that also shies away from discomfort at all costs. I was just a heartbroken kid who thought she drove her mother away because she was unlovable. That wasn't true, but I wouldn't have the courage to examine and heal that belief until I was 38. The backdrop to my heartache was that as I mentioned, my genetics didn't give me a naturally thin body. But now there is a medication that will help me with that if I want, and the judgment I have about myself is now optional. I never knew the judgment part was optional, until I started earnestly practicing self-kindness.

Writing out your Struggle Story will help you separate the challenging events that happened to you from the self-made judgments you attached to how you live your life and make decisions. It's part of deconstructing and reconstructing your relationship with your body and food. So, let's get started.

Get Ready to Unpack Your Struggle Story
Like many stories, there are usually elements of truth and fiction. How often those lines become blurred in the human experience is surprising. How you see your body, your relationship with food, and all of your

experiences are blends of many memories and often contain very real things that happened to you that may have been hard and traumatic. So, as you start to unpack your story, be kind and gentle and start with the small stuff that doesn't spin you into emotional dysregulation. When I began unpacking mine, I started with small events first and then left the hardest ones for last. With a courageous heart that gained confidence over time, I finally became ready to look at the events I had boxed up in my heart and tucked away, left to collect dust in a corner.

Writing out your Struggle Story helps you start separating feelings from beliefs, which can help you shift your focus from changing your feelings to changing your beliefs, which is doable and the most effective route for healing your relationship with food and your body. Emotional eating is a common coping mechanism we've developed to help us handle the big waves of emotions we experience that we don't quite know what to do with. After a while it can become second nature and our primary coping mechanism.

Why Unearth the Past?
This book aims to shine your self-compassion onto the misunderstandings still running the show. Most of us have them and don't even realize it. Hidden deep in the unconscious, deeply held beliefs feel true... but aren't. Those beliefs are still the primary drivers of your relationship with food and your body. And, up until now, you've been wrestling with those drivers in some way, thinking that mindset, mental strength, and sheer willpower were the ways to tackle and change them. But they don't work because they don't have the magic element of self-kindness in them—they have the aspect of punishment. You've probably been looking for the "right" method, just like you've most likely been looking for the "right" diet to magically unlock the secret to a body you'd finally find happiness with.

Because of the continual exhaustion and subsequent failure of our ability to tackle body and food problems, it's natural to stow away our past and never look at it again. While GLP-1 medications are opening the door, they aren't powerful enough to do the transformational work to change the misconceptions about our innate goodness. But they can help us get unstuck from the stories that run so deep and so loud that we don't know anything else. Unearthing their stories with the help of mental space while on a GLP-1 has proven effective for many of my clients. It's like when people go on an anti-anxiety medication, and they can start looking at their anxiety because they are less overwhelmed. We have to bring the untrue narratives you are running to the surface, so you can learn to try a new way—and that requires you to revisit them.

Exercise: Writing Your Struggle Story

Write down some challenging events from the last few years. They can be something that happened directly or indirectly to you.

Examples:

My company downsized, and my workload increased by 50 percent.

A neighbor started a construction project that was very disruptive to surrounding neighbors.

My mother was diagnosed with dementia.

I pulled my shoulder muscle at the gym, which kept me from exercising for a month.

I got into an argument with my brother, and we stopped talking to each other.

How did you feel about each of your struggles? What emotions did you experience with each? Take time to write what feels true to you about these events.

Examples:

I felt so overwhelmed by all the work I had.

I felt unappreciated by my neighbor.

I felt grief-stricken about my mom.

I felt annoyed about my shoulder.

I felt angry at my brother and felt hopeless.

Now, review what you wrote and determine if you have started to believe something about yourself or life due to your struggles.

Examples:

I was not a valuable member at my job, or else they wouldn't have done that.

My neighbors don't care about me.

Everyone who I love leaves me.

My body is against me.

I'm not a priority for my brother.

Review what you wrote. Take note of the difference between what you experienced, how you felt about it, and what you decided. If you'd like, repeat this process a few times with different events. You may start seeing themes or patterns in the takeaways of your experiences. We will revisit this in the next chapter and expand this process. This is the beginning of understanding the deeper pieces of our work together. We can't change what happened to us, but we can change what we decided about ourselves after the event, which really keeps us stuck and emotionally dysregulated, especially around food.

Kendra's Struggle Story

Here's an example of how this storytelling can help while on a GLP-1. My client Kendra had been on Monjaro for six months. During that time, she experienced an improvement in her weight as well as reduced hunger. This was a welcome change; her hunger finally felt manageable after it had felt out of control for so long. Not only was it manageable, but also it had essentially become a non-issue. This boosted her confidence after so many years of feeling deep shame around food—often feeling like she was a failure for not being "strong" enough to control her cravings. On a call together, Kendra shared that after her most recent shot, the food noise seemed to creep back in a bit; it was noticeable during a stressful project at work when she found herself leaning back into urges to binge to handle work stress.

Immediately, old fears came flooding back: "What if the medication stopped working? All my progress will be lost." She immediately reverted to an old pattern of belief that she would never be good enough and felt that old familiar feeling of needing to be perfect to feel safe. Those untrue beliefs resurfaced that "permanent peace with food and her body was simply too good to be true" and that it would be her fault. On our call together, Kendra was able to write her struggle story and articulate how this event helped unpack the bigger story at play (insecurities about herself and lack of inner strength). I suggested that the fear of that happening was not to punish her but as an opportunity to heal it.

Kendra's Struggle Story:
- Challenging event: Felt food noise creeping back after her recent shot

- Her feelings about the event: Scared, let down, confused
- What she believed about herself regarding the event: She would never heal her relationship with food or her body, GLP-1 meds were too good to be true, and the progress she thought she had made wasn't real.

It was new for Kendra to see her experience through a framework that allowed her to separate feelings from beliefs. Like so many of us, Kendra focused on changing her feelings to feel better rather than her beliefs. This is an epidemic in our world. We live in a world that continually shies away from discomfort and actively avoids confronting deeper issues. It's common (and natural) to be overwhelmed by feelings and keep our focus on managing the overwhelm that comes with those feelings instead of facing our beliefs, so I don't blame anyone for wanting the discomfort to just disappear rather than facing it. Humans have developed effective and often elaborate ways to skirt discomfort, such as scrolling on our phones, eating, and binge-watching TV. Kendra wasn't aware of her beliefs because they seemed so second nature to her. In fact, they were so second nature it didn't occur to her that they may not be true and could be changed. In Kendra's case, when she started to understand this, it helped make sense of the quick reaction when the food noise temporarily returned. Beliefs are harder to change than pushing away feelings, but it's an effort well spent because it's where real change occurs.

Struggle Stories Help Us See Our Obsession with Fixing Our "Wrongs"
You've likely tried many times (and for many years) to silence the constant food-related chatter in your mind, because not only is it a nuisance and a distraction, but also our culture tells us it's wrong and unhealthy to think about food so much. Kendra's story is an example of how food noise is not only an unwanted guest but also, oddly, a way to understand her Struggle Story when she stopped judging food noise and paid attention to it in a different way than she was used to. Remember, Kendra was convinced her beliefs were true because they had been around for so long and that her feelings of being scared, let-down, and confused were in her power to eliminate if she just tried hard enough. But when she reframed food noise from "bad" to "curious," it allowed her to map

out her Struggle Story and became a treasure map of sorts for Kendra to understand more about herself.

Unfortunately, our society endlessly sends signals that reinforce the lie that *we* are wrong, our feelings are wrong, and we are in charge of fixing that "wrongness" by being perfect. Not being able to get our hunger and thoughts about eating under control is an example of this. This is very unfortunate, because many who suffer from the disease of obesity judge how much they think about food, believing it's something in their control. From books and magazines to podcasts and practitioners, we're bombarded with a laundry list of "just-dos" aimed at changing our relationship with food:

- Learn to control your hunger.
- Eat only natural foods.
- Adjust your mindset.
- Create "healthy swaps" for your comfort foods.
- Unlearn unhealthy eating habits.
- Try intuitive eating.
- Stop intuitive eating.
- Go vegan/keto/carnivore...
- Be "mentally strong"/have willpower.
- Take medication as needed.

Rightness about health is pervasive in our society, and for a seemingly good reason: Who doesn't want to do what "they" say should be done to improve our well-being? Few of us are experts, so we look to the people and sources around us who are perceived to be thought leaders and fountains of knowledge for cues about what we should or should not be doing to heal. It's natural, and even wise, to seek information and evidence to support our decisions, especially when caring for ourselves. Trying to "be on the right side" also saves us time (life hack, anyone?) and potential embarrassment (who wants to look uninformed?) while giving us a sense of authority and confidence in our choices.

At the same time, fixing is something of a national pastime these days, especially when it comes to eating, diet, health, and wellness. We lean into every "right" we uncover, because if we could just make that one change, all would be well. We avoid all the "wrongs" we hear about, because those drag us down and keep us stuck where we don't want to be. Increase willpower? Check! Eat intuitively? Check! Go vegan? Check!

Adjust mindset? Books read and class taken. Check and check! Keto instead of vegan? Check! Portion control? Check! Stop eating intuitively? Check! The list quite literally never ends.

Another pervasive message is that "mental strength" is one of the "right" answers. It isn't, though, and has, in fact, been proven to be ineffective. An interesting study done in 2022 examined female wrestlers who emotionally ate, looking for a link between mental toughness and emotional eating. What it uncovered was that as female wrestlers' mental toughness increased, they tended to eat emotionally and feel guilty about it. While it was a small study, it really debunks the notion I repeatedly see, which is that willpower to "just put down the fork" fixes eating issues.

All of this has been magnified a hundredfold in recent years. We're surrounded by messages, information, and screens—filled with programs, studies, recipes, classes, diets, and more—that separate our foods, activities, actions, thoughts, and so on, into "good" and "bad" categories. If you dip a toe into social media these days, you'll likely be met with a barrage of posts and videos on food, eating, and finding peace with both. The aggressive tribalism that's developed around diet culture and anti-diet culture is almost unavoidable.

I've often thought, *I just want to know the right thing to do to care for myself.* To my slight embarrassment, if Google gave me a feedback report on the hours I've spent researching seed oils, protein bars, exercise routines, and intermittent fasting plans, it would likely reveal weeks, months, or even years of my life dedicated to these pursuits. I used to harshly judge the time I spent researching food, supplements, health fads, and scientific articles or the amount of physical space supplements, books, and how-to guides have taken on my kitchen shelves. My inner perfectionist insisted that if I were truly healthy I'd research but not excessively, eat healthy without obsession, and maintain a practical focus on well-being while ignoring any body-image concerns. As unrealistic as that is, we rarely let go of these out-of-reach ideals entirely, fearing that doing so would lead to overindulgence and a lack of discipline.

While well-intentioned, rightness and fixing simply don't adequately address the core relationship we have with food and our bodies. They're superficial, mind-based responses to what is, in fact, a deeply rooted struggle that lives in your heart. Smaller portions might shrink your waistline, but they don't touch internal views of your own self-worth. GLP-1 medications might quiet your food noise, but they don't correct or alter the beliefs about yourself that inform your intuition. New eating habits might improve your BMI, but those new habits will be short-lived if built on a belief that you're undeserving.

How much we think about food and eating is often seen as something that needs to be fixed—a problem we need to find a solution to. It isn't. It's a powerful signal to extend care and kindness to the hurting parts deep within us to discover the story unique to you and the journey you are taking. Addressing this pain by becoming conscious of your Struggle Story eliminates the need for fixes and ushers in the freedom to choose a way to live and eat that truly feels good.

Trying to "Fix" Our Emotional Eating

Not everyone who goes on a GLP-1 medication is an emotional eater. But most of us (whether on a GLP-1 medication or not) emotionally eat on occasion. Emotional eating—using food to cope with emotions rather than to satisfy physical hunger—is one of the most common forms of food struggle. In reaction to stress, anxiety, depression, boredom, and/or loneliness, emotional eaters look to food as their balm of choice. The foods they frequently turn to are high in sugar, fat, and/or salt; these foods release feel-good chemicals such as dopamine, serotonin, and endorphins in the brain. And for those who struggle with the disease of obesity, satiety signals in the brain are often skewed, making it not only challenging to determine if you are hungry or full but also easier to emotionally eat because of those skewed signals. I bring it up here because so often, whether we emotionally eat or not has become a yardstick of judgment toward ourselves, and it perpetuates the myths that if we don't emotionally eat, we are good/right, and if we do, we are bad/wrong. This not only can create a Struggle Story but can also perpetuate others as well.

Ella's story

Ella's parents divorced when she was eight years old. She lived with her mother, who had remarried. Her new stepfather was emotionally abusive, regularly drank alcohol, and verbally berated the family. Her mother,

Kathy, worked two jobs, and to handle all the emotional stress that came along with her life, she never missed daily exercising and religiously counted calories to stay at a specific body weight. Ella observed this and wondered if she should exercise and count calories like her mom. As a backdrop to this, Ella was experiencing tremendous ongoing sadness about her parents' divorce. She couldn't understand why her father, who had remarried and had a new baby with his wife, didn't make time for her.

To cope, Ella retreated into reading books, staying quiet, and getting out of the way of her volatile stepfather, and she did not overly demand her mother's precious little time after work. She found that reading and snacking alone in her room helped alleviate the stress she had no idea how to fix. She was sad that her mother worked so much and didn't have time to spend with her. She was also sad about her father's continual absence from her life. She felt lost, lonely, passed over, and unimportant.

This continued into high school. She became painfully shy, overweight, and filled with anxiety she had no idea how to handle—except by snacking alone in her room at night. One day, in a class at school, she learned about mindful eating and realized that uncovering her emotions around food had little to do with willpower or knowing the "right" way to eat. She discovered how to become aware of her feelings while she ate. She was startled at how much sadness drove her to eat when she noticed it. Before this, she simply saw it as a way to manage overwhelming feelings. After weeks of practice, she noticed that her emotions around food had softened and that she often ate to cope with her sadness. This was a revelation to Ella. She also began experimenting by noticing her hunger and fullness cues, which she was unaware of before.

Her relationship with food improved. Her anxiety improved. She even noticed that her metabolism had shifted. She felt empowered about her relationship with food. For the first time, Ella felt hopeful that her habits and shyness might not define her.

A few years later, Ella was interviewing for her first job after graduating from college. In general, her stress eating had improved. She had learned ways to soothe herself that didn't include food, and she felt like she had put all the childhood anguish behind her. She got the job and moved to a new city. She was excited, scared, and nervous. The new job presented new challenges like having a new boss, work performance reviews and running meetings. A month into her new job, she started having panic attacks—seemingly out of the blue. Logically, she knew that graduating college, moving to a new city, and starting a new life were a lot of changes to handle, so anxiety might be a part of it, but she was still surprised by this new development.

To cope with her anxiety, Ella found a therapist, went on Wellbutrin, and started yoga, which seemed to help a bit. A few months later, though, she was still having panic attacks and started developing hypervigilance around her anxiety to prevent a panic attack. She found herself becoming more reclusive and declining social invitations from her co-workers for fear she might have a panic attack. She leaned back into snacking in the evenings and eating more to temper the stress from the anxiety she felt no control over. Suddenly, mindful eating wasn't working for her anymore. Fast forward six months, Ella had gained 30 pounds and was diagnosed with Type 2 diabetes. Her doctor put her on Ozempic, and she slowly started losing weight. Being less hungry stopped the emotional eating, and she didn't gravitate to stress eating, but still, her anxiety and panic attacks persisted. Why?

The big change in Ella's life uncovered the belief framework that mindful and intuitive eating never solved back in high school: that who she was at her core caused her to be passed over and unimportant to her parents. The truth depends on your perspective, and in Ella's case, her truth was she wasn't worth anyone's time or energy.. She used lifestyle "fixes" that temporarily helped until life challenged her to look deeper at these perceived truths and beliefs. She also believed she had years of proof that her assessment of herself was correct. Her father wasn't a big part of her life, and her mother didn't make time for her. But here's an interesting thing: Caring is bigger than being right, and care for herself hadn't been tried yet—only fixing. Although Ozempic radically improved the surface level of how food helped her cope, it didn't get to the true root of beliefs driving her poor self-image and all the ways she continually tried to fix herself.

Ella believed it wasn't safe to share who she was in her new job and adult life because of the deep fear that people would leave her, just like her mom and dad did. Her inner compass was set to that setting, so everything revolved around those beliefs, even though she outwardly changed her relationship with food. Ella believed that staying small and out of the way kept her safe, so her life organized itself around that belief. She tried to change this, understanding to some degree the limitations it placed on her. She worked to control her anxiety and make peace with food, but those early compass settings from her childhood remained. Largely unaware of these core beliefs and their influence, Ella didn't know how to reorient her internal compass.

Are We Trying to Fix Our Struggle Stories with Bad Data?
Renowned podcaster and bestselling author Glennon Doyle once described her journey with eating-disorder recovery by saying, "I'm just trying to be less fucked up." This blunt admission struck a chord with me, echoing my feelings before I embraced self-compassion and reparenting. Glennon's position (which is one I hear a lot) is that she's fucked up and that needs to be fixed. The starting point of her journey with food is correcting being fucked up. It takes a lot of energy to be less fucked up and, most important, it's not true—it's just part of her Struggle Story. Like many of my clients, I had spent excessive time trying to "fix" what I thought was broken in me without questioning if I was actually broken. I just assumed I was, given the overwhelming anxiety and pain in my life.

The assumption that I was broken turned into a belief that set the tone for all of my life decisions. Assumptions often become beliefs and then become the central narrative of life, an example of using "bad data" around food and eating. Furthermore, bad data that forms beliefs halts emotional growth. We become "stuck" in the emotional growth age when we experience trauma and form our beliefs, carrying the unprocessed pain and limiting perspectives of that time into our adult lives. For decades, I focused on having the "correct" tools to compensate for believing I was broken rather than correcting my bad data. This is the single biggest problem I see around food issues: trying to fix the symptoms instead of addressing the root cause. In my case, I became laser-focused on removing the emotional pain of my childhood instead of looking at my bad data perpetuating my Struggle Story and believing I could soothe and nurture hurting parts inside me. I can't help but wonder how many people like me, like Glennon, and maybe like you, are working on fixing things they believe about themselves that aren't actually true.

Many of my clients express similar confusion about how to remove and fix emotional

pain instead of exploring how food has been used as a stand-in to do that, and how they can do it without food. We need to explore solutions, not fixes. Here's the difference: A fix is typically a more immediate, often temporary, answer to a specific problem, especially regarding repairs or corrections. It implies a response to something that is broken, malfunctioning, or not performing as expected. A fix might not address the underlying cause of a problem but rather patch it up to make it work for the time being. A solution is an answer to a problem or a means of effectively dealing with a difficulty or challenge. Solutions can be temporary or permanent and can range from simple to complex. Unlike a fix, a solution often implies a more comprehensive or fundamental approach to resolving an issue, potentially addressing the root cause. The difference between the two terms often lies in the depth and permanence of the response to a problem. A fix is a quick and specific response, while a solution is generally more comprehensive and aimed at fully resolving an issue for the longer term.

We will focus on using self-compassion and reparenting to build a solution (not a fix) for

your struggles with food. This approach will help you understand that your Struggle Story is not a problem; it's a guide that you can follow to build trust, wisdom, and resilience inside yourself. Struggle Stories point us to the metaphorical splinters we all have that get in the way of peace around food and our body, so we can pull them out and start healing.

Examples of Fixes vs. Solutions
Fix: avoiding difficult conversations or pretending disagreements don't exist
Solution: engaging in open and honest communication to address underlying issues and work toward mutual understanding and resolution

Fix: relying on credit cards or payday loans to cover recurring expenses
Solution: creating a budget, increasing income, or reducing spending to address financial challenges

Fix: trying to numb or suppress difficult emotions like sadness, anger, or fear

Solution: allowing yourself to feel and process emotions with self-compassion, validating your feelings, and offering yourself comfort and support

Fix: following a strict, highly restrictive diet and exercise plan to lose weight quickly for an upcoming event
Solution: creating a sustainable, balanced workout routine and nutrition plan that align with your individual goals and lifestyle for long-term health and fitness

Fix: taking over-the-counter medications to suppress symptoms of a chronic illness
Solution: addressing the root cause of the illness through lifestyle changes, medical intervention, and ongoing management to improve overall health and well-being

Shifting from Acceptance to Cooperation

One of the best ways to move from the fixing mentality to a heart-centered solution is to practice approaching your Struggle Story as a journey that you are cooperating with rather than a problem you are fixing and accepting. Notice how you feel in your body when you consider switching from acceptance to cooperation and trust.

The idea of radical acceptance has always really bugged me. The concept sounds appealing but putting it into practice is where things become challenging. The concept of acceptance creates a feeling inside of me that screams "your wants and needs don't matter—just get out of the way and go with the flow of what the universe is presenting you with!" It has a flavor of "just take your medicine and shut up." But humans aren't wired that way. We have egos, opinions, and preferences.

Ever had a mole checked for cancer at the dermatologist? I have, and you bet I had a preference that it be non-cancerous. So, let's say the mole comes back cancerous. Do we just accept it? *Yes, but there's more to it.* Cooperation with your circumstances is the missing piece. When we cooperate, we accept what is but add a secret sauce: We enter a space where we actively allow our preferences to be part of how we create a plan. Acceptance becomes a collaborative effort between ourselves and the universe. Cooperation says "we are doing this together." Me and the universe, together, collaborating, exchanging ideas, sharing preferences.

Cooperation creates less resistance because humans thrive when they are part of the creative process. We want agency, not just surrender. I've found this to be a very important concept both in my own life for anything challenging I face, and for those who are struggling with issues around food and their body.

* * *

Many of us live in a polarized landscape that makes it hard to truly heal our relationship with food. There is a focus on fixing ourselves and aligning with a group mentality to heal. Those are short-lived. To move beyond this polarized landscape, we can shift our focus inward and look for the experiences that shape our relationship with eating. This journey of self-discovery allows us to make informed choices about how to care for our bodies, regardless of societal pressures or prevailing narratives. By honoring our individual needs and preferences, we can cultivate a healthier and more sustainable relationship with food and our bodies, embracing what some call body autonomy or what I simply refer to as personal choice.

Your relationship with food and your body isn't a defect in need of repair. It's a powerful signal to extend care and kindness to the hurting parts deep within you and a personalized map to the inner folds of your heart, which contains the truth: You are whole and good, and pain is a symptom of being cut off from that truth. Addressing this pain by discovering your Struggle Story and knowing this truth eliminates the need for fixes. If we could take some moments and stop judging our eating and instead ask, "What is my relationship with food helping me understand about myself?" it becomes a tool instead of a problem to fix. I like this approach because I often hear many suggestions for "unlearning" diet culture. Words like dismantle, break up, recover, protect against, and ditch are also used in reference to diet culture. This language can send the message that you learned the wrong thing (which you should correct) or missed the "correct" information. The message when you hear that you need to "unlearn" diet culture is that you should set your inner compass straight. Oddly, it's the opposite of trusting yourself and your experiences.

What if the way you eat was guiding you inward to trust yourself and everything you learned? Encouraging you to listen to the whispers inside your heart and to turn toward the places inside you that may be confused, scared, curious, and alone and have used food to help find a connection? From that perspective, no unlearning is necessary—and all learning is helpful. In this way, you can explore your relationship with emotional eating, use it to help you identify your Struggle Story, and ultimately unearth some of the untrue beliefs that need healing.

Chapter Takeaways

- Taking the time to write out your Struggle Story can help you understand your story and create clarity, so it's easier to discern feelings from beliefs, which helps discover the root of your relationship with food and your body.
- The immense pressure to "fix" and be "right" in our approach to eating and health is aimed at saving time and energy, but it can make us feel that we are "wrong" when we can't get our hunger or thoughts about eating under control.
- Assumptions often become beliefs and then become the central narrative of life, an example of using "bad data" around food and eating.
- Shifting from "accepting and fixing" to "cooperating and trusting" can create a space where we can explore what our Struggle Story is here to teach us about ourselves and our beliefs.

Chapter 2

What Happened to You... and What Do You Believe?

I was once spiritually ill—we all pass through that—but one day the intelligence in my soul cured that. —Meister Eckhart

As we all know, life is not a straight line upward. It's filled with twists and turns, steep inclines, and massive drops. Close bonds form and dissolve. Successes and failures happen every year. Joy and sadness are both present. Whether it's things we perceive as big (the birth of a child, a significant promotion at work, the divorce of parents) or relatively small (being stood up by a date, scoring the winning point in a tennis match, killing our fifth—and final—house plant), each of these events leaves a footprint in our hearts and minds.

Beliefs play a significant role in the relationship we have with food, our body, and life itself. Often deeply ingrained from childhood events, cultural messages, or personal traumas, beliefs act as filters through which we interpret our experiences, influencing how we respond to words or actions, react to situations, and perpetually feel in our own skin. Critically, some (many?) of the foundational beliefs we have about ourselves are simply wrong, providing us with bad data that subconsciously impacts our lives in ways both big and small.

In this chapter, we will delve deeper into your Struggle Story and examine how it often shapes your worldview and settles into the unconscious. You'll identify false beliefs you hold about yourself and explore how they might impact your relationship with food and your journey with GLP-1 medications. And you'll learn how to adjust these beliefs through the strength of your heart.

How Beliefs and Memories Are Formed—and Can Be Transformed
Our beliefs about ourselves, the world, food, and health are deeply rooted ideas and assumptions shaped by our upbringing and social environment. These beliefs can be positive or negative, and they often operate on both conscious and subconscious levels. For example, a negative experience like failing a class in school might lead someone to believe they are unintelligent or inherently a failure. During that period of failing a class, someone may be aware (consciously) of feeling like a failure. Then, over time, the brain naturally shifts that belief into the subconscious, where it becomes less accessible to the conscious awareness, to make room for new experiences and beliefs.

It's estimated that we are only aware of 5 percent of what the brain is doing.[1] Thus, 95 percent of what we operate from is largely subconscious—out of our awareness but built on the "programming" we have had until that point. Beliefs about food, for instance, are deeply intertwined with our core beliefs about ourselves: our value, lovability, and worthiness. These core beliefs are often formed unconsciously and can be difficult to change because they reside in our subconscious. We tend to categorize these beliefs, once formed, as either "good" or "bad" and tuck them away, where they continue to influence our relationship with food and self-worth, often locking us into rigid patterns of thought and behavior around food.

But what if the beliefs underpinning our actions and food choices are untrue?

Because most beliefs are largely out of view of our own awareness, when we experience stress and feel isolated, our brains store those memories and the beliefs arising from those experiences in a spot that's tough to access. This leads to moments when something triggers these memories, and we find ourselves reacting in ways we don't like and struggle to control. This is particularly evident with our relationship with food, which often seems to take control automatically, leaving us feeling powerless.

How does this happen?

---

[1] Brainz Magazine, "The Subconscious Mind's Role in Influencing Your Behavior," *Brainz Magazine,* accessed [Date You Accessed the Article], https://www.brainzmagazine.com/post/the-subconscious-mind-s-role-in-influencing-your-behavior.

Initially, beliefs are conscious thoughts ("Ouch, that feedback from my boss hurt to hear; maybe I'm not really good at my job like I thought"), but regardless of being correct or incorrect, they move into our subconscious, where long-term memory is stored. Thus, "I am not really good at my job" becomes the emotional intuitive groundwork for how we find future jobs, receive feedback from work reviews, and view ourselves at work. These beliefs, whether true or not, live in the subconscious and make up our intuition. Our intuition may tell us we have to try extra hard to get a job to compensate for the belief that we aren't a good worker. This is an important point to make, because we may be unaware that the beliefs forming our intuition are then molding our relationship with food, our body, and emotions. Emotional resilience—the ability to bounce back, adapt, and cope with adversity without negative side effects—is the superpower we can learn that helps us discern in the moment whether a belief is true or not, so it doesn't go on to get stored in long-term memory as truth.

Memory Reconsolidation

We've established how experiences can create beliefs, and how beliefs— whether true or not—can be put into subconscious memory and continue to dictate how we make decisions and form relationships. This is called memory consolidation. It's like collecting memories from our experiences and storing them away in our mind. When we recall events in our life, we "think back" to them, much like looking up old photos in an album.

Yet memories are more than just mental snapshots stored in a single brain location; they're woven into our entire being: mind, body, and heart. When we recall old memories, they can evoke a powerful physical and emotional response, even years later. For instance, when I remember getting into a car accident in fourth grade, I can still feel the confusion, fear, and pain. It can feel like we are destined to forever associate life's hardest moments with those negative associations.

But there's hope. We can actually rewire those old memories through a process called *memory reconsolidation.* Memory reconsolidation allows us to take old memories with painful associations and change them, linking them to neutral or even positive feelings. This is especially relevant when it comes to food and body image. For example, many people use food to cope with stress, creating a strong association between food and emotional regulation. Memory reconsolidation offers a way to transform those associations, leading to a more peaceful relationship with food. It can feel incredibly hopeful to know that we may not be destined to retain negative associations with our hardest life experiences.

Memory reconsolidation is the process in which we recall a memory, and with intention, modify it by infusing it with kindness. Consequently, when it gets stored back into long-term memory and is recalled at a later date, it doesn't have the negative emotional charge associated with it. Because memories aren't fixed, each time we revisit a memory, there's an opportunity for change. More than that, it is quite simple to do with practice, and while you can do it with a therapist, you can also do it by yourself by implementing self-kindness and care.

Infusing a memory with self-kindness could be as simple as associating a difficult memory with a new thought and feeling: "You were doing the best that you could" or "Wow, I am so proud you got through that!" Recalling a memory from a place of self-kindness over time ensures that these memories are solidly anchored from a place of abundance, not lack. Even though we cannot change what happened to us, we have the power to change what we decide about ourselves. Each of us can transform our relationship with our memories and ourselves.

It turns out that hard relationships with food and our body, while seemingly an endless challenge, is actually a persistent signal urging us to care for and be with these parts of ourselves. Doing so will not only resolve the things we believe are holding us back from peace and happiness in all areas of our lives, but it will also grant us access to our compassionate hearts, the ultimate internal healing resource.

Let's take a closer look at what happened to you, the beliefs that emerged, and how that created a worldview. We'll examine how your habits can be an attempt to compensate for the pain these beliefs cause, and we'll explore how, by addressing and then transforming these beliefs, you can break free from the negative viewpoints you have about yourself and find lasting healing. Doing so will help to prepare you for bumps in the road with GLP-1 like handling the fear that might creep in that food noise is coming back, or if for whatever reason you have to discontinue use. Taking the time to proactively examine your belief system will help prevent old patterns from emerging as you prepare for post-GLP-1 life, especially now if your food noise is quiet.

Beliefs: Protectors That Are Not Always Accurate

We hold beliefs as true within ourselves, organizing our lives and our self-perception. They provide the foundation to make sense of the world. Yet even though we regard beliefs as factual evidence, they are not necessarily so. While some of them are accurate, many—particularly those at the heart of the relationship we have with food and our body— are not. But given the significant emotional safety component in beliefs, they can feel very true, even when they are not.

I recall my student Claire, for instance, who found it challenging to discuss the pain of growing up with a binge-eating disorder because doing so felt like a betrayal of loyalty to her mother and father, whom she loved very much. She was truly grateful for how they had provided for her both emotionally and financially, so criticizing them in any way felt like a betrayal of their generosity. Deep down, though, she felt anger that they hadn't supported her when she was bullied at school, which eventually lead to her binge eating. They often seemed more focused on smoothing things over and keeping up good appearances with friends and family rather than advocating for her. Claire believed that bringing into the open her struggle with food meant she wasn't grateful for her parent's generosity, and this belief obstructed her ability to express and process natural anger, an essential step in her recovery. Beliefs are often embedded so deeply within us that they are hard to recognize, but we also tend to defend them with convincing arguments that seem valid.

Untrue beliefs often stem from misunderstandings in challenging circumstances. *When faced with challenges, we frequently assume that we are the problem.* Our self-criticism doesn't stop at thoughts like "You aren't good enough" or "You should be trying harder." Instead, we go further, drawing hard lines in the sand about our innate worth. We elevate the negative phrases we hear or believe to gospel truth, such as "You are worthless" and "You will always be a failure." *Misunderstandings become truths.* Then, as adults attempting to untangle the web of emotional eating and make peace with food, we overlook the "You are worthless" belief as a misunderstanding and instead hold it as truth.

The table opposite lists some common examples:

Situation	Untrue Belief That Formed as a Result
My father was absent.	I am unlovable.
I was abandoned as a baby.	Something is wrong with me.
I was diagnosed with cancer.	God is punishing me.
My Parkinson's disease is worsening.	I'm doing something wrong.
I can't stop binge eating.	I am weak.
I was fired from my job.	I am worthless—a fraud.
My husband cheated on me.	I am ugly and boring.
I can't lose weight.	I am a failure.

While we can outgrow beliefs to an extent, simply stating, "I release that belief," doesn't prompt immediate change, since these beliefs were survival mechanisms. Our society often promotes a 'mind over matter' mentality that fails to acknowledge how deeply ingrained these harmful self-perceptions are, nor does it equip us with the tools to fundamentally change our beliefs about ourselves.

Untrue beliefs:

- keep us emotionally safe
- help us make sense of challenging life events.
- can be passed down through generations by our ancestors
- are built on a foundation of lack
- often cannot be removed simply through the power of the mind or willpower
- can be transformed through your care and presence

Here's an example from my own life. As I've mentioned, my parents divorced when I was six years old. Back then, in the eighties, therapy wasn't typical, and as motherless girls, my sister and I did not process our grief over our parents' divorce with a trained professional. The subsequent months were marked by anger, sadness, and helplessness, which eventually led to a self-imposed silence, my way of regaining control.

With hindsight, I realize that simply attempting to fix the pain was less effective than understanding what I had decided about myself due to that life event. Unlike the unchangeable event itself, these self-perceptions were mutable. Beliefs formed from this experience included:

- I am a throwaway kid.
- I don't matter.
- I am not worth the fight for my mother to keep me.
- I am unlovable.
- I could have persuaded my mom not to leave me if I had been smarter.
- There must be something wrong with me because my mother abandoned me.

These beliefs formed the underpinning of my first food binge in the second grade and the first diet I initiated when I was nine. Being motherless made me feel inadequate, and I yearned for solace, comfort, perfection, and love. Manipulating food and my body was a feasible way to achieve these. However, I hadn't realized then that self-kindness and recognition of my pain were what I truly needed and were the transformative balm to a peaceful life.

Fast-forward to the dissolution of my first marriage. This event allowed me to confront the pain caused by my mother's absence and the underlying beliefs that had shaped me. Until then, I had merely created life scenarios designed to prove my lovability and sought relationships that offered me a semblance of safety. Safety I assumed was outside of me—in a place I could find if I tried hard enough. But, to truly understand my relationship with food, career, relationships, and family, I needed to delve *into* my experiences and, crucially, understand the beliefs formed.

I had not made the connection before; it wasn't just the trauma of my mother leaving me that was the root of my pain and anxiety. It was the belief that I was unlovable, insignificant, and a throwaway child that kept me locked in a cycle I was desperately trying to break free from. But what I needed in order to course correct from my shame cycle of untrue beliefs was never taught to me in school or church or by books, multiple therapists, energy workers, or wise and loving friends. Learning to be kind to myself, paired with reparenting, allowed me to catch and care for myself as I fell into the doom spiral of thinking and then believing I was unlovable. It gave me a felt experience of safety and balanced my nervous system, so I knew that I could handle harder things when they came my way. It took time and practice to build this internal trust that I could provide safety for myself.

Erin's Story

Erin grew up in a large family and often felt lost in the family dynamic, needing more attention than she received. She felt unimportant in a family full of boisterous, loud siblings. There was a lot of competition for love, attention, and belonging. She grew up thinking she wasn't the person anyone in her family wanted, and to help with the feelings around this, she binged on food.

Eventually, Erin married a wonderful man who was kind, caring, and loving. He worked long hours out of town, and she found herself bingeing on food after he left for work to handle the stress of his absence. She knew logically that he wasn't trying to punish her or make her feel unimportant. But she felt an old familiar feeling of loneliness when he left and secretly wished he would find a job where he wouldn't be away so much. She turned her judgment inward each time he left, wondering why he chose this job and wasn't choosing her, just like when she was a child competing for attention and belonging in her big, overachieving family.

Erin felt driven to figure this out and heal her bingeing, so she was open to counseling and came to see me. She had always seen bingeing as a problem to get over, solve, and get past. She saw it as a flaw in herself that contributed to why she had to convince people she loved to show her attention. One day, I gently suggested that bingeing was here to show her she had her "math" wrong. All this time, she thought she was the problem (she was attempting to solve her "problem" with bad data about her worth), but she hadn't done anything wrong. She just thought she had because of how painful it was to live in a family that constantly made her feel like an outsider. To make sense of the pain she felt as a result of her family situation, she internalized the blame, convinced that somehow she was responsible for this happening. As a result, her life set up a framework based around that self-blame.

After working together for a while, I suggested she might have a mix-up happening that she didn't realize; I suggested that bingeing was present in her life to guide her to the part inside of her that believed (incorrectly) that she was the problem. Perhaps bingeing wouldn't give up on her until she gave up the idea/belief that she was the issue and traveled inward to care deeply and mother the part of her that felt lost, scared, confused, and passed over. Erin kept waiting for her family, relationships, and career to show her that she was worth the attention of others—outside validation of her worth—but that wasn't happening. She then used that as fuel for her story and to blame herself: "See? They didn't put you first! Proof there is something wrong with you!" Then a binge would come on to soften the blow of those beliefs.

But Erin was a deeply caring, loving person who was determined to heal. I kept flipping the story to help her see that her story and belief system may not have her best interests in mind. Bingeing wasn't the flaw to correct; rather, it was a road map to follow into her heart to see where she had incorrect assumptions about herself due to the emotional pain she suffered as a child. The entire purpose of bingeing could be to help her love that sad, lonely girl who just wanted attention from her family. I suggested that the next time she had the urge to binge, she pause for a moment to see if there was an opening for her to acknowledge that little girl and ask her what she needs. When she engaged her imagination and did that, she discovered that her little girl just wanted adult Erin to spend time with her and put her first, just like she wanted her family and partner to spend time with her and make her feel like she was a priority.

Erin's story illustrates how innocently and how often we come to untrue conclusions about ourselves, how that causes separation from our innate goodness, how we try to compensate for an issue inside of ourselves with outside validation, and how that can create a framework of daily life. She had been working on this for years, trying to change her mindset and learn techniques to overcome her bingeing. But bingeing kept her engaged—not to punish her, but to alert her to the bad data she was using to run her life; she was unaware of it because our culture tells us that we are at fault in most circumstances. Life will repeat the opportunity to care for ourselves over and over and over again, and in Erin's case, it came with her journey of bingeing. Being on a GLP-1 medication creates mental space and calm from the noise of constantly thinking about food as comfort whether you're using food to soothe pain or to satisfy hunger you might feel, so you can take advantage of the opportunity to examine those deeper beliefs.

How to Change Your Beliefs

Now let's shift to what *you* can do to increase your awareness of your beliefs—and then change them. The more you can become conscious of your beliefs, the more accessible they become so you can collapse them. You can start a daily practice to discover them and also cultivate kindness toward yourself for needing to believe these beliefs to keep yourself safe. Practice saying caring statements toward yourself and your beliefs like "I am so sorry you had to believe this to stay safe. You didn't do anything wrong. I love you." Notice how it feels to extend kindness to your beliefs. And try the following exercise, which will help you deeply explore how your beliefs came to be in the first place.

Exercise: What Happened to You... and What Did You Decide?

The best way to understand how beliefs may play a positive or negative role in your life is to write about them. In this exercise, you're going to explore events you've experienced and the beliefs that came to life because of them. It's important to include both big and small events, even though you may not perceive them as having been particularly challenging.

List five to ten personal challenges. Think about the challenging events you have faced, and write down several that stand out in your mind. Note your age at the time of each event.

Detail each event. Describe how each event impacted you and how you felt. Be as specific as possible.

Identify resulting beliefs. Reflect on what you believe about yourself as a result of each event. Be specific.

Step 1 Example: Challenging Events

- Six years old, parents divorced
- Ten years old, bullied at school
- Twelve years old, dropped by friend group at the start of summer
- Fifteen years old, had to move to a new city because of my dad's job
- Sixteen years old, experienced my first relationship and breakup
- Twenty-one years old, moved to NYC for a job and got fired six months later
- Twenty-three years old, experienced a miscarriage and a breakup and moved back home

Next, revisit each item you listed and consider the feelings and challenges of the experience. Write down how that event changed you. (Note: You might identify multiple changes as the result of a single event.)

Step 2 Example: How the Events Affected You
- Six years old, parents divorced
- Became the emotional caretaker of my mom; had to grow up fast; experienced first feelings of sadness and loneliness
- Ten years old, bullied at school
- Started experiencing crippling stomachaches; felt extreme anxiety about going to school; school was no longer safe, fun, or enjoyable
- Twenty-three years old, experienced a miscarriage and a breakup and moved back home
- Became clinically depressed; gained twenty pounds; felt extreme hopelessness; had no direction or purpose in life

Review each item on your list and consider what you have written so far. Write down what you decided about yourself after each event.

Step 3 Example: What You Believe
- Six years old, parents divorced
- Became the emotional caretaker of my mom; had to grow up fast; experienced first feelings of sadness and loneliness
- My needs are unimportant in my family. No one will be there for me. I'm responsible for my mother's well-being. Life is scary and disappointing.
- Ten years old, bullied at school
- Started experiencing crippling stomachaches; felt extreme anxiety about going to school; school was no longer safe, fun, or enjoyable
- Something is wrong with me. I must be perfect to be safe. No place is safe.
- Twenty-three years old, experienced a miscarriage and a breakup and moved back home
- Became clinically depressed; gained twenty pounds; felt extreme hopelessness; had no direction or purpose in life
- Life is full of disappointments. I'm doomed to be punished and tricked by life. I don't deserve happiness. I am unlovable. Food is my only safe haven.

Once you have completed listing and analyzing your events, take a moment to reflect deeply on the beliefs you formed from these experiences. Consider whether these beliefs still resonate with you and how they manifest in your current behavior and thoughts. Are you surprised by any realizations? Examine how these beliefs have influenced your decisions, relationships, and overall outlook on life. Assess their validity: Are they based on past misconceptions or emotional responses? By understanding and accepting these beliefs with compassion, you can start the journey toward healing and a more balanced life. Ask yourself, "what would it take for me to change my beliefs?" How does it feel to consider the idea that you can change your beliefs with a change of heart instead of a change of mind? Stop for a moment and take a breath and notice how it feels to do this.

* * *

We often dwell on the events that have occurred in our lives and their immediate impacts, such as becoming the emotional caretaker for a parent after a divorce. However, we may not fully acknowledge the underlying beliefs these experiences instill, like feeling that our needs are secondary or that we're alone in our struggles. This oversight occurs because of the following reasons:

- Most healing approaches don't effectively address how to change beliefs.
- Many people are unaware of the beliefs driving their lives in the first place.
- Beliefs tend to move into the unconscious mind if not addressed at the time they were formed, becoming invisible and largely unrecognized despite their profound impact.

At the heart of every false belief lies a moment that caused us to turn away from our true selves, often out of a need for self-preservation. To cope with the pain, we may adopt an untrue narrative, creating an emotional shield that protects us from further suffering.

These false beliefs, formed for emotional safety but based on misunderstandings, frequently persist into adulthood and impact various aspects of our lives, including our relationship with food. They act as an unconscious lens, influencing our decisions, self-worth, and perception of ourselves.

We often define ourselves by the perceived flaws these beliefs suggest, such as "I am a victim" or "I will always be unlovable," rather than by our true nature. This doesn't negate the reality of victimization or feelings of unlovability but highlights how we tend to internalize these experiences as core aspects of our identity, rather than recognizing them as temporary states or external circumstances.

By acknowledging and addressing these false beliefs with compassion and understanding, we can break free from their limiting influence. Through meeting, examining, welcoming, caring for, and being with the parts of ourselves that harbor these beliefs, we can learn to regulate our nervous system independently, freeing ourselves from the need to rely on food or other coping mechanisms.

Chapter Takeaways
- Our beliefs are shaped by our experiences, moved into our subconscious, and influence our relationship with food and self-worth, even though these beliefs are often untrue.
- Memory reconsolidation is a way to take memories with bad associations and reassign them with our own care.
- A hard relationship with food and our body is actually a signal urging us to care for and be with the parts of ourselves that are hurting.
- Given the significant emotional safety component in beliefs, they can feel very true, even when they are not.
- By understanding and accepting your beliefs with compassion, you can start the journey toward healing and a more balanced life.

Chapter 3

How Many Life Jackets Are You Wearing?

The greatest sources of suffering are the lies we tell ourselves.
—Bessel van der Kolk, *The Body Keeps the Score*

Beliefs are powerful forces that drive behavior, whether true or untrue, conscious or unconscious. They deeply impact our lives, often without our awareness. They are always present, touching everything we think and do, feel and want, while influencing the decisions we make and how we interact with the world around us. And they persist regardless of being on a GLP-1 medication or not.

When formed during periods of adversity or challenge, they can take on special significance that can protect in the immediate term but hinder in the longer term. Over the years, they can accumulate like layers, one on top of the other, sometimes reinforcing already existing beliefs and other times in direct conflict with beliefs established previously.

When beliefs solidify and intertwine in times of distress, they become what I call Life Jackets, offering much-needed (lifesaving, even) safety and protection during stormy periods. They shield us from emotional, spiritual, and physical anguish, helping us navigate difficult situations and rationalize challenges. For example, a person who grew up experiencing significant financial insecurity develops the belief that "you must save every penny and never take financial risks." This belief served as a Life Jacket during their impoverished childhood, helping them maximize limited resources. However, as an adult with stable finances, this same belief prevents them from making sound investments or reasonable purchases that would improve their quality of life. Even while taking GLP-1 medication and experiencing success with weight management, they might obsessively count pennies saved on groceries rather than celebrating their health improvements.

But what happens after a given storm passes and the Life Jacket we put on is no longer needed? The majority of us do nothing. We simply move forward wearing that Life Jacket in perpetuity until the next storm arrives, at which point we make another Life Jacket and put that one on too. This process repeats itself, until we're wearing Life Jacket on top of Life Jacket on top of Life Jacket. In the process, what originally served as a vital tool for survival oftentimes transforms into a burdensome hindrance that limits our freedom, growth, and well-being, while stopping us from embracing life fully. Experiencing the quieting of thoughts in your brain while being on a GLP-1 medication is a profound opportunity to look for and remove Life Jackets, so that you can finally heal your relationship with food and feel peace with your body.

Sometimes, life beckons us to reach for more—a relationship, a career goal, healing of some kind—and our Life Jackets get in the way, so we have to take them off to get to where we want to go. To do so, we will have to use our hearts, believe in ourselves, and recognize our inner goodness. In this chapter, we're going to look at the Life Jackets we're carrying and explore how we can use the power of our hearts to identify and remove the ones that inhibit our healing.

The Utility and Limitations of Life Jackets

Imagine if someone asked you to walk around wearing five actual life jackets on a hot summer day. How would you change your day to accommodate the many unnecessary layers? What would you avoid doing? How would you feel doing something as simple as walking down the street? How would the life jackets alter your perspective on the world? What impact would they have on your abilities?

Now, consider the potential impact of belief-based Life Jackets— invisible, but no less burdensome. How many are you wearing right now? How are they influencing the actions you take in a day? Or the relationships you have? What about the way in which you view yourself? Do they alter the choices you make or the paths you walk?

The following chart lists examples of beliefs born of adversity and the Life Jacket narratives formed as a result to protect us from the harsh waters of life and to calm the nervous system. We often wear these Life Jackets for years and don't even realize it. They might have been incredibly effective at shielding us from pain or hurt at the outset, but in the wrong context—and when layered one on top of another—they can become unbelievably heavy weights that make living freely very challenging.

Belief	Life Jacket
"I must have provoked that reaction."	Blaming Myself Life Jacket. Protects you from feeling hurt by others but also makes you feel responsible for things that aren't your fault.
"There's something inherently wrong with me."	Broken Life Jacket. Keeps you safe from having to believe in yourself but also traps you in feeling bad about yourself.
"If I'm perfect, maybe the abuse will stop."	Perfection Life Jacket. Gives you hope that you can control bad things but also makes you feel like you're never good enough.
"I can only earn their love if I'm flawless."	Needing to Be Perfect to Be Loved Life Jacket. Protects you from feeling rejected but also makes it hard to have real, close relationships.
"It's my fault. I need to fix it."	Fixer-Upper Life Jacket. Helps you make sense of challenges but also makes you feel overwhelmed and responsible for things you can't control.
"I can't trust anyone. I'll get hurt."	Lonely Life Jacket. Keeps you safe from getting hurt but also stops you from making close connections with people.

Everyone has Life Jackets. They aren't our fault; we didn't mess anything up by creating them. Most of us wear multiple Life Jackets, a testament to our resilience in overcoming hardships. These protective layers become so integral to our existence that discerning them becomes difficult. And since they were initially worn for protection, shedding them feels counterintuitive, even when we cognitively recognize that they hinder personal growth. They are silent strategies that assist us and are deeply integrated into our eating. *They were formed at a time when we were doing the very best we could with the resources we had.* Each time we take a bite of food and think about the why and how behind that bite, we usually do it with a Life Jacket on and have no idea.

We often attempt to repair the emotional "damage" caused by these events through therapy, the perfect diet, fulfilling careers, relationships, or sheer willpower. For some, food acts as a buffer against our pain, while others find solace in controlling their physical appearance. Unfortunately, these solutions are often temporary and unsustainable. Our nervous system retains memories of our trauma, ranging from sudden shocks like the death of a parent to sustained stresses such as living with a verbally abusive guardian.

Over time, these ingrained misconceptions solidify, making them challenging to discard. But here's my groundbreaking proposition: Life beckons you to rediscover your intrinsic value. It prompts you to understand that not only are you safe but expressing your love is safe too. Struggles with food are a manifestation of life urging you to reclaim this truth.

Kate's Story

Kate grew up with an overbearing mother and father. As with all her siblings, she felt forced to live up to their high expectations. But Kate's body was naturally bigger than those of her brothers and sisters, which over time caused her to believe that her body was less attractive than theirs and that she might have been born defective in comparison. Her mother struggled with body image too but had used chronic dieting to handle it. Her father worked long hours and was emotionally checked out most of the time, except when he was yelling at everyone to "do better, try harder."

Because Kate's mother was always dieting, her fear of food spilled over into Kate's life. From a young age, Kate knew the nutritional value of most foods and knew how to deprive herself if she found she had gained a bit of weight. To compensate for her hunger and the small amount of food she ate, she learned how to binge food in secret so she wouldn't get caught by her mother and be chastised. Her mother openly spoke to others about Kate's "food rules" and even forced her to have Diet Coke and frozen yogurt while her siblings had regular Coke and ice cream.

As she grew older, Kate developed disordered eating, stretches of restricting and bingeing, a struggle she kept hidden until after her college years. She repeatedly tried and failed to stop, admonishing herself with the belief that a genuine desire for healing would enable her to quit. Unbeknownst to her, underlying her disordered eating was the belief that food provided solace more effectively than she could provide for herself. Her self-hatred developed from her inability to embody the "do better, try harder" family mantra about her body size that seemed to work for everyone in the family but her. Without a conscious understanding of this misguided coping mechanism, no solution to her bingeing seemed to last.

Moreover, Kate harbored a belief that something was fundamentally wrong with her, a notion that took root after she grew up not being allowed to eat normal food and feeling left out of many normal experiences. Bingeing served as both a punishment for her perceived "wrongness" and a balm for the self-directed anger stemming from it. Even though her friends told her she was amazing and beautiful, she still held the idea that she was fatally flawed deep inside, and she held herself in near-constant judgment about her inability to control her eating or find a happy medium around food.

Giving up bingeing on food meant no comfort, but eating food meant constant judgment directed at herself, so that pushed her into restricting. Kate found herself in an endless yo-yo cycle and felt powerless to find a true solution. Finding the "perfect" diet or developing a healthier mindset seemed an easier and more logical solution than looking at the pain she was constantly running from. She had convinced herself that she had a food problem, but she didn't. She had a self-value problem that she was trying to solve through food. Even when she tried intuitive eating, Kate felt completely out of control. She had no idea that her belief system and the multiple Life Jackets she wore kept her in the constant push-pull that kept her nervous system dysregulated. The Life Jackets would stay put until she could care for the parts inside of her that believed she was wrong and transform her false beliefs with care, compassion, and presence.

Kate's doctor prescribed Zepbound for her weight and sleep apnea. Within three months, she had lost almost 40 pounds, and for the first time since she was a child, she wasn't thinking about food around the clock, and she completely stopped bingeing and restricting food. Truly, it seemed that her Life Jackets had been removed, and food had permanently taken a back seat in her life. The push-pull was gone, the constant thinking was gone, the search for the "perfect" diet was gone, and she just lived her life without the food elephant in the room. But, unfortunately, Kate was laid off from her job and her health insurance was discontinued. When that happened, her Zepbound prescription was no longer covered. Unable to afford the out-of-pocket cost, she had to abruptly stop the medication. This created a spiral in Kate's mental health after she felt the food noise returning after a month. Hunger and thoughts about food took over, and she started to notice the weight creeping back. She had been so convinced that her issues with food had been healed for good, but they hadn't. Panicked, she reached out to me to see if there was a way to make sense of what was happening and stop the uncontrollable (yet familiar) feeling returning.

When Kate came to see me, I had her write out her Struggle Story and the belief system that resulted from it, and then I had her identify the Life Jackets that were holding her down, and here's what we discovered:

> **Life Jacket 1:** Who I am and how I was built is wrong, so I'm going to implement various ways to show that I can look "right," like forcing my body to look smaller.
> **Life Jacket 2:** I must try ten times harder than everyone else for the same results, so I'm going to use bingeing to get relief from how hard I have to work.
> **Life Jacket 3:** Eating like a regular person in front of others is not safe, so I'm going to eat the way that feels regular to me in secret.

Her Life Jackets were one of the main reasons she was panicking about having to manage life without the help of Zepbound. The more Life Jackets she had, the further she was from being in touch with her inner essence and intuition and could trust herself, instead of using food to manage stress from life and her beliefs. Of course, examining and removing Life Jackets does not guarantee food and body freedom, but it does reorient our coping skills to be from an abundance source (trusting ourselves, having self-value) rather than a lack source (using food to cope) and gives the best shot for healthy habits. Life Jackets direct intuition to keep us safe even though over time they become burdensome. Life Jackets were made to protect our hearts, so we also use our hearts to take them off. No matter what has happened, our hearts can still identify and remove the strategies that Life Jackets provide us. The only requirements are care, curiosity, and willingness.

Kate came to see how Life Jackets form from multiple beliefs born of difficult experiences. Challenging events can lead us to believe untrue things about ourselves, and these beliefs create a Life Jacket, which becomes a strategy for moving through life. For Kate, it started with the high expectations she wasn't sure she could meet because she lived in a bigger body, causing her to question if she was born defective. This impacted her body image, but the family narrative was "do better, try harder," so she implemented lifestyle tactics to mold herself into what she thought would be more socially acceptable based on her belief. She created a Life Jacket strategy (bingeing to compensate for her hunger, dieting to "do better, try harder") to make sense of challenging circumstances and make herself look like she wasn't born defective. If she started bingeing, dieting, and "trying harder" again after Zepbound, she was convinced she would be left with proof of the painful (un)truth of "I was born defective" that she thought was behind her, and she faced what felt like a double loss. Her relationship with food wasn't actually healed and the easy solution—being on Zepbound—was being taken away.

On top of that, she had no idea how to reconcile that within her family system, without making things feel worse or abandoning family loyalty. It seemed easier for Kate to return to her old ways, restricting food to mold into the family's acceptable narrative rather than face the pain of feeling born defective and the massive letdown that Zepbound was too good to be true. What she didn't know then, but understood after, was that she could do something about the predicament she found herself in through the power of her heart.

As we worked together, we reviewed many of her beliefs, and she confirmed that what we discovered resonated with her. However, she was surprised to hear these beliefs articulated aloud, as is often the case with my clients. Discovering these underlying beliefs can be startling, and Kate was taken aback to realize that something so apparent in our conversation had been unknowingly influencing her daily eating habits. Clearly understanding these beliefs (her Life Jackets) proved invaluable, as it gave her a focal point for applying compassion and reparenting skills.

Upon further discussion, Kate shared that many of the Life Jackets were created after an accumulation of beliefs had formed when she was around seven years old and had solidified when she was teased by her siblings for wearing a swimsuit on a summer vacation. The beliefs she formed would have seemed logical and helped dampen the pain at such a young age. She also realized that her eating today (before Zepbound) was directly dictated by beliefs from long ago, and she was ready to release them. This was a brilliant discovery. Kate had the power inside of herself to heal the drivers of disordered eating. While she couldn't change that she had lost her health insurance and thus her Zepbound prescription, she could change the role of food and body image, so she was better prepared for having the ability to lessen food noise by reclaiming the truth: She was lovable, valuable, and wasn't made "wrong."

Sometimes, learning what Life Jackets you wear can help lift them. Other times, it takes more time and compassion. In Kate's case, whenever she wanted to binge or restrict food, she took the time to move into her compassionate heart, remember her seven-year-old self who had few resources, and imagine caring for her. She would take a breath, then ask that little girl what she needed and imagine giving it to her. She would also recite, "I forgive myself for believing that food soothes pain better than I can," when she felt the urge to binge or restrict. Over time, Kate's eating habits improved. She began to understand how her disordered eating was a form of hiding the real pain she felt, and she spent weeks asking her younger self what she needed to feel safe, loved, and connected. Kate regularly set aside time to imagine loving the parts of her that struggled with food at different ages; she imagined hugging them, holding their hand, and telling them she would always be with them. Kate now sees her relationship with food as a vehicle that taught her to truly care for and love herself, reminding her that she will never be alone.

Kate found that she could identify and remove her Life Jackets and, more important, uncover their purpose. This understanding allowed her to learn about herself and develop wisdom. She ultimately discovered how to support herself in a body that societal and family norms told her wasn't as good—which was untrue. On her journey with food and Zepbound, Kate uncovered a powerful truth: She was not wrong or horrible for bingeing and restricting. Bingeing and restricting were a guidepost signaling that she had the ability to self-care in a different way if she chose to. She could uncover the beliefs woven into her Life Jackets and do something about them. When she embraced the inner work of tending to the pain in her heart, she no longer needed to binge, for she had found safety inside herself, along with the recognition that her heart was there to comfort, guide, and heal her. Eventually, Kate landed a new job, new insurance, and was able to go back on Zepbound. This time, however, she wasn't afraid that if she had to discontinue the medication, she would find herself back in an old, painful place. She trusted that she could support herself no matter where life took her.

Exercise: What Are Your Life Jackets?

Life Jackets are hiding in plain sight. It often only takes a short conversation with my clients to uncover the Life Jackets they wear. The easiest way to understand what Life Jacket you are wearing is to talk and write about your life and then listen and read what you wrote. You may need to try this a few times, but know that your stories are inside of you, waiting to be told.

Remember the exercise in the last chapter: "What Happened to You... and What Did You Decide?" You may have discovered some beliefs you created for good reason. Let's take that further here and see how your beliefs may have formed into Life Jackets.

Here are some prompts so you can practice listening to yourself to discover your Life Jackets:

1. Take a moment to take a few breaths. Bring forward feelings of compassion, curiosity, and care, even if you have to think about a person or pet you love.
2. Remember an event that was a challenge in your life.
3. Write a few paragraphs describing the event and how you felt about it.

4. What were your biggest takeaways from that event about you and your life? List at least ten.
5. Look at each item in your takeaway list one by one.
6. Are they beliefs?
7. Ask yourself, "Do I believe that [insert your takeaway]?
8. Take a moment to reflect and be honest with yourself. Have these been long-standing beliefs that felt true?

Remember, beliefs are woven into the very fabric of our relationship with food and ourselves. They likely seem true because, at the time they were formed, they provided a logical way to cope with emotional pain. However, they are not truths but mere placeholders.

Exercise: How to Remove Your Life Jackets

The most straightforward way to remove Life Jackets is to become aware of them and, with deep caring and compassion, forgive yourself for creating and believing them at a time when you were doing the best you could. Many of the Life Jackets we wear have been with us for years, and remember, it takes time, trust, and courage to remove them. They are shed with the same level of safety and care as we used to create them. Some Life Jackets will come off quite quickly and easily; others will be with us longer than we'd like but will become lighter and lighter as we lovingly become aware of how their presence is an attempt to protect us.

Your heart recognizes Life Jackets because your heart placed them there to begin with to keep you safe, but now is the time to release them. As you begin this exercise, take a few centering breaths and imagine moving into your heart space.

Here are several mantras I say to remove Life Jackets:

- "I forgive myself for believing _____."
- "I forgive myself for judging myself for believing _____."
- "I am so sorry we had to do it this way and believe _____."
- "Peace be with you."
- "I love you, and I am so sorry."
- "I forgive myself for believing that I was unlovable."
- "I forgive myself for believing that I have to try ten times harder than everyone else to get the results I want and for believing that I was made wrong."
- "I forgive myself for believing I have to be perfect to be safe."

Remember, forgiving yourself for believing something that seemed true isn't about letting anyone else off the hook for their actions; it's about allowing yourself to become free of something that is getting in the way of what you are ready to accomplish. When we become aware of deeply held beliefs that cause dysregulating emotions, we tap into the body's ability to calm and regulate itself.

> Tip: If you find yourself jumping from diet to diet, searching for ways to be healthier or eat healthier, consider how you judge your inability to find just the right path. Jumping from diet to diet is a way to discover what Life Jackets you wear; it's not about your inability to find the correct path.

* * *

Most of us wear several Life Jackets. The more we have on, the harder it will be to choose "healthy" foods or eat "in moderation" because our nervous system defaults to safety first and seemingly "healthy" eating advice second—or, for some of us, not at all. Just like actual life jackets keep us from drowning, belief-based Life Jackets shield us from drowning in emotional pain.

But you can start working on your personal Life Jackets by becoming curious about what yours are, how many you might have, and why you needed them. You can also be gentle with yourself if you find that you're wearing a few, because they were put in place to help you make sense of difficult experiences. Know that your heart is stronger than your Life Jackets, so when you feel comfortable using your heart to stay safe, you'll be ready to let go of your Life Jackets.

Chapter Takeaways

- We devise survival strategies called Life Jackets and, in the process, form misconceptions about our self-worth to shield ourselves from feeling big, hard emotions that mold our identity and help us survive.
- Life Jackets are composed of multiple beliefs that help us survive hard things, but over time they become strategies we use even after the hard thing is over. They are silent strategies that assist us and are deeply integrated into our eating.

- Self-kindness and understanding are made of a stronger material than Life Jackets, so they are an effective tool for removal.
- Our hearts can still identify and remove the strategies that Life Jackets provide us. The only requirements are care, curiosity, and willingness.
- The more Life Jackets we have on, the harder it will be to choose "healthy" foods or eat in moderation, because our nervous system defaults to safety first.
- Being on a GLP-1 medication is a profound opportunity to look for and remove Life Jackets, so you can finally heal your relationship with food and feel peace with your body.

Chapter 4

The Power of Self-Compassion

All darkness vanished, when I saw the Lamp within my heart.
—Kabir

Self-compassion is a radical act of kindness and support toward oneself, especially when facing suffering, pain, or mistakes. In more tangible terms, it means treating ourselves the same way we would a close friend who's made a mistake or is struggling: gently, kindly, and with care.

Self-compassion is a self-generated form of emotional and spiritual safety. Practicing it has been shown to improve your emotional resilience, body image, and self-view, while also being emotionally protective. Equally valuable, you can call upon it at any time and at zero cost, allowing you to access safety from within, rather than from lifestyle, diet, or community. It's often more difficult to implement than people imagine, because it can be surprisingly hard for people to be kind toward themselves, and it must be actively called upon to have impact. It may be easier to begin learning and practicing self-compassion while you're on a GLP-1 and may be experiencing a bit of a break from the usual thoughts about food and your perceived "failures." In this chapter, we're going to explore the meaning of self-compassion, consider the science behind it, and begin developing a practice for immediate application.

The Three Elements of Self-Compassion
In her 2011 book, *Self-Compassion: The Proven Power of Being Kind to Yourself*, Dr. Kristin Neff provides an eloquent definition of self-compassion, asserting that it comprises three elements:

1. **Self-kindness:** extending kindness toward ourselves
2. **Common humanity:** recognizing that suffering is a universal human experience
3. **Mindfulness:** being present with our experiences, thoughts, and beliefs to facilitate their transformation

Self-compassion is an abundance-based model of living, rooted in the idea that our worth is inherent in our humanity and that nothing we do can take away from it (even when we make mistakes). Because of this, self-compassion boldly declares, "I deserve love and kindness simply because I exist."

In its highest form, self-compassion expands the truth that we are already and always whole. The human experience becomes a journey of remembering this wholeness through life's challenges, instead of a path of continual self-persecution to explain life's challenges. This practice encourages us to embrace our present suffering instead of pushing it away, while illuminating where we've unconsciously separated ourselves from our values, goodness, and love. It's a heart-guided, soul-supporting approach to caring for ourselves, no matter the circumstances.

The recipe for self-compassion requires you to have these three ingredients:

1. **Willingness** – to be kind to yourself and bring care into the present moment
2. **Imagination** – to create a picture in your mind of being kind to yourself (Form follows thought, so imagine what it looks like to connect with and be kind to the parts of yourself and what it looks like to engage your compassionate heart.)
3. **Caring-Tenderness** – the action of loving support (This can often be thought of as turning on the compassionate part of your heart or the place inside you that activates when you deeply care for someone else: an action, word, or phrase of kindness.)

By engaging willingness, imagination, and love, a person can start the inner engines of self-compassion. The same is true for many other human experiences like finding a job or navigating a health challenge—we must act with intention for the experience. By first intending to be self-compassionate through imagination and willingness, we bring self-compassion forward so we can experience it.

Self-Compassion vs. Empathy vs. Self-Esteem

Although self-compassion has been widely studied, it is also often misunderstood. Many clients I work with, for example, improperly conflate self-compassion with empathy—two abilities/skills so distinct that they use different parts of the brain. Others mistake self-compassion with self-esteem.

Self-compassion centers around the truth that every human is born whole, and nothing that happens to us in life takes away our wholeness, even though it may feel otherwise. Derived from the Latin *com* and *passio*, meaning "to suffer together," self-compassion directs us to be kind to ourselves and incorporates a belief that we can help.

Empathy, on the other hand, is the ability to understand and share the feelings and pain of others. When we empathize, we feel someone's suffering and with that may experience their pain vicariously, leading to emotional distress and fatigue. In fact, MRI scans have shown that empathy activates areas in the brain involved with processing threat or pain, such as the amygdala.[2] While empathy is essential for connection and understanding, if it is not balanced with self-care, it can be emotionally taxing and can contribute to burnout, called empathic distress. This could potentially lead to seeking comfort in food for emotional release.

Meanwhile, self-esteem is a measure of confidence in one's worth or abilities. Built on the notion of things going our way—inwardly and/or outwardly—self-esteem is predicated on there being a standard of "success" against which we can compare ourselves and to which we may aspire. Things like getting a promotion, praise/accolades from friends and colleagues, social media likes, and so on can drive self-esteem. But when those things vanish or fail, we have nothing to compare ourselves to except our failure. Self-compassion isn't based on a measure or comparison; it supports us in any state we find ourselves in and says we are worthy of kindness because we are alive. This is especially important because so much of our relationship with food tends to be built upon rewarding or punishing ourselves based on how life is going.

---

[2] T. Bertram et al., "Human Threat Circuits: Threats of Pain, Aggressive Conspecific, and Predator Elicit Distinct BOLD Activations in the Amygdala and Hypothalamus," *Frontiers in Psychiatry* 13 (2023): 1063238, https://doi.org/10.3389/fpsyt.2022.1063238.

For instance, if you find yourself within your goal weight, you may reward yourself with a special treat. If, however, you step on the scale and you weigh more than you did the day before, you may skip a meal or, alternatively, eat five desserts to soothe the feelings of defeat. In a self-esteem construct, you might swing from feeling accomplished for having reached your goal to feeling like an abject failure for having regressed. Self-compassion, on the other hand, allows you to care for yourself in all circumstances, whether you've reached your goal or strayed from it. Self-compassion is the best trick up your sleeve, because it provides consistency in how you treat yourself regardless of outcomes. It lets you acknowledge setbacks without harsh judgement, celebrate progress without attaching your worth to it, and maintain a balanced perspective throughout your GLP-1 journey. Rather than riding the emotional rollercoaster of achievement and failure, self-compassion offers a steady hand of understanding that helps you make choices from a place of care rather than criticism or temporary emotion.

Self-Compassion, Eating, and Body Image
Research consistently shows that being kind to yourself—practicing self-compassion—can dramatically improve your relationship with food and your body. This approach is especially valuable for those on GLP-1 medications, where physical changes often outpace emotional adjustments. What I can tell you without reservation is that the more you learn and practice self-compassion, the better off you will be as a person, and especially a person on a GLP-1 journey, navigating its peaks and valleys.

Self-compassion means treating yourself with the same kindness you'd offer a good friend during difficult moments. Rather than harsh self-judgment (the pastime of our culture!) about your body or eating habits, you learn to respond with understanding and care. Studies reveal that people with higher self-compassion experience significantly fewer disordered eating behaviors and body image concerns.[3] This gentler approach creates a foundation for healing that medication alone cannot provide.

---

[3] Turk, F., & Waller, G. (2020). "Is self-compassion relevant to the pathology and treatment of eating and body image concerns? A systematic review and meta-analysis." *Clinical Psychology Review,* 79, 101856

According to numerous studies in recent years, self-compassion offers many benefits surrounding food, body, and eating struggles, such as:

- buffering against eating pathology
- preventing onset and relapse of eating disorders
- reducing eating disorder symptomology
- increasing motivation, body image, and body satisfaction
- being more effective than cognitive behavior therapy in some cases, like binge eating disorder, for those who have experienced trauma
- reducing binge eating frequency
- increasing psychological health
- reducing the tendency for self-criticism, shame, depression, anxiety, rumination, thought suppression, perfectionism, and disordered eating attitudes

By reminding us of our wholeness, self-compassion transforms challenges with food and our body into pathways for remembering that we're always lovable—even if society tells us we have "flaws" that need to be fixed. In the process of rediscovering our wholeness, self-compassion becomes a mechanism for liberation that allows us to address the underlying beliefs, judgments, and stories we've constructed to separate ourselves from our inner goodness.

Restating something mentioned earlier in this book, we can't change what happened to us, but we can change what we decide about what happened to us. Research by Yuki Miyagawa, Yu Niiya, and Junichi Taniguchi in 2020[4] found that self-compassion helps people view failures as learning opportunities rather than something to be avoided. This means that even though we can't change our past experiences or failures, we can use self-compassion to change how we think about them, viewing failures as stepping stones toward growth, rather than as poor reflections on our inherent worth or abilities. Shifts in our perspective can significantly impact the beliefs we hold as true. The best part? Your thoughts, feelings, opinions, and habits around food can significantly improve.

---

[4] Miyagawa, Yuki, Yu Niiya, and Junichi Taniguchi. 2020. "When Life Gives You Lemons, Make Lemonade: Self-Compassion Increases Positive Self-Evaluation After Imagined Failure." *Japanese Psychological Research* 62, no. 1 (January): 39–50. https://doi.org/10.1111/jpr.12265.

Moreover, self-compassion helps us cultivate internal resilience. Defined as "the ability to recover from or adjust easily to misfortune or change," resilience plays a pivotal role in the lives of those with food challenges. Inward kindness softens the impact of trying circumstances by reminding us of our humanity. It also frees us and our actions from judgment, dismantling the shame, guilt, and self-blame often associated with food struggles and emotional eating. As a result, self-compassion helps protect against developing and relapsing disordered eating and improves body image, body awareness, and positivity, allowing us to live a life aligned with our own values and not shun experiences for fear of doing something "wrong."

The Epidemic of Shame

Shame is a poison that has spread around the world and invaded the hearts of many. It's the number one driver of issues around food and body that I encounter personally and professionally. Shame and self-blame are the sentiments I hear most frequently from clients who struggle with food. Shame frames the internal dialogue as "I am wrong," rather than "I did something wrong," while self-blame lays all responsibility for actions and outcomes onto the emotional eaters themselves. Individually, neither is helpful or accurate. In combination, they lock people into existing patterns and habits while crystallizing destructive feelings. We use food to soothe ourselves because we believe that we're broken, damaged, and/or wrong, in turn reinforcing our already-faulty views that we're broken, damaged, and/or wrong.

The spider web of shame surrounding each area of the GLP-1 movement is real—because of the very harsh eyes of society that for some reason is looking down on those who take it, and because those who take it often already feel shame. Why is shame so pervasive in our current culture? Because there are so many hurting people. Hurting people turn against themselves in an attempt to make sense of their pain, and that trait is passed down through families.

It's so pervasive that it touches almost every person I've met, including me. Growing up I thought I was damaged in some way because my mother didn't raise me, so therefore I was unlovable. That framework (I'm unlovable) was what my childhood brain conjured up to make sense of the pain as a result of an absent parent. Believing this as a child both helped me compartmentalize the pain and was the source of shame. I believed *I* was made wrong/unlovable and that war I waged on my own lack of value was a constant sword of shame stabbing me over and over again. Here's the kicker: I didn't think this was abnormal. It just seemed like fact, probably because I was so young when my shame formed. My mother was just a young abuse survivor who didn't have the capacity to be a responsible parent. At six years old, I couldn't understand something complex or nuanced like "your parent just doesn't have the capacity. It's them, not you."

The "Oh, wait, this is all happening because I'm unlovable" framework helped me structure reality to be less overwhelming but at the same time made *me* wrong instead of seeing the situation as painful and messed up. That innocent misinterpretation on my part kept me locked in a shame cycle for years. Decades even! Shame sneaks up on us because it seems logical at first. It gives us breathing room around emotional pain. But so often we just adapt to it and integrate it into the reality of who we think we are and then develop elaborate ways to compensate for it like eating, body dysmorphia, and toxic relationships. And then we walk around in the world shaming others to help mute the shame we hold for ourselves. That is what is happening right now as we enter into the new GLP-1 era.

Shame is when we believe we are the problem and, therefore, unworthy. Shame develops as a result of really anything hard or challenging happening in our lives that causes us to turn against ourselves in some way. The problem with shame is that it freezes emotional growth, because to grow we need to believe we have value. It prevents us from evolving emotionally and spiritually and from reaching for more in life and taking the risk to evolve. It's the ultimate deal-killer and body-image destroyer. The good news is that self-compassion is the antidote to shame.

For those on GLP-1 medications, it may seem like you are jumping from one steaming pile of shame crap to another—living in a body that is in itself a challenge for personal reasons and moving onto challenges that society is putting on you that somehow taking a GLP-1 medication is cheating, a sign that you lack willpower and can't control your out-of-control relationship with food. Anti-diet proponents are saying now that GLP-1 medications are a medicated avenue to control one's body that perpetuates the inherently fat-phobic culture we live in. Others say that you should learn to control your cravings and just eat healthy and exercise. Still others say these medications perpetuate eating disorder behavior that can mimic anorexia. Honestly, WTAF. I mean, society tells us we just can't win or be happy without thinking that we are cheating or flawed—and that's shame woven so deeply into our culture we can't even see it. Shame lurks around every corner in our society, and I say there is real value in looking inward and sorting out what is driving the shame in you instead of what society is saying.

So, what heals shame? You do. Your heart does. Self-compassion does. Remembering the world is a bunch of hurting people who are continuing to hurt others to help their own hurt. Reminding yourself that very, very hard situations tend to make us turn on ourselves and decide horrible things but we have the power to reverse it. Full stop. No one can heal your shame but you. The world will try to convince you that power, money, fame, a perfect body, great health habits, and perfectly straight white teeth will heal you out of a shame cycle, but they will not.

Self-Compassion Is Rewarding

Self-compassion stimulates reward centers in the brain—the very centers stimulated when we eat. Research shows that compassion activates the brain's reward system, releasing feel-good chemicals like dopamine and oxytocin, promoting positive emotions without the need for food. This creates a positive feedback loop that fosters resilience, motivation, and emotional well-being. This would be especially true for those on GLP-1 medications who can't eat to reward themselves due to a decreased appetite and may be looking to other sources to increase feel-good neurotransmitters.

Self-Compassion Is Simple—but Not Easy

When I first encountered the concept of self-compassion, I had practiced compassion, meditation, and mindfulness for many years. I hadn't explicitly directed compassion inwardly, however, because I naively and arrogantly thought that being kind to myself was not only a no-brainer but a simple approach for which I was already too advanced. I couldn't have been more wrong: It's proven to be one of the hardest things I've ever done.

Self-compassion is simple—but it isn't easy. There's a very straightforward question at the heart of self-compassion: *How would I treat a friend in this situation?* When applied inwardly, the answer to this question becomes the kindness and self-care that defines self-compassion. It turns out, however, that humans have a *really* hard time directing kindness toward themselves. Our default setting seems to be somewhere between "self-persecution" and "self-flagellation," so we typically punish ourselves for our struggles much more aggressively and rapidly than we show ourselves warmth and compassion. This is especially true when it comes to emotional eating and body issues.

Imagine supporting a close friend going through cancer treatment. You'd likely have no trouble coming up with a list of kind things you could do or say: texting encouraging words, bringing food to their house, going to doctor's appointments, creating a space for them to discuss how scared they are. . . . You'd lead with care, kindness, and words of encouragement.

Yet when we think of being kind to ourselves in the same way, the struggle becomes very real very quickly. When I raise this paradox with clients, most worry that practicing self-compassion around food and eating equates to weakness and giving in to their food urges. Moreover, practicing self-compassion requires that they admit their suffering, struggle, or hurt. This vulnerability can be extremely challenging and uncomfortable, particularly for those who have spent decades building walls to make sure their darkest, most hurt parts didn't get seen. Also, some fear that creating a safe place for their hurt parts could allow those parts to "take over."

Here's what my clients worry about the most in regard to self-compassion and eating:

- Showing kindness will allow their most "broken" parts to come forward and run their lives, and they will lose control.
- Acknowledging and connecting with the internal places they struggle with will make them look weak and out of control, worsening things.
- Being kind to the part of themselves struggling with food will permit those struggling parts to take over and could even cause mental instability.
- They will lose themselves in the process of deeply caring for themselves.
- Their hearts aren't strong enough to be kind to themselves.

Almost any approach like self-compassion with a mindfulness component will illicit fears like this. It's normal, expected, and part of the process. Placing emphasis on the heart instead of the mind will set off warning signs, because the mind likes ultimate control. The mind also operates from a "glass is half empty" and "control danger at all costs" model, so it's useful to know that when you bring in the transformative power of the heart, you may hear warning bells.

Meghan's Story

Meghan, a confident extrovert, came to me in a panic. She'd been on a GLP-1 medication and recently hit a stall in her weight loss. The stall triggered intense anxiety: What if the medication had stopped working? Was she missing something? Was it her fault? Should she eat less? Try harder? Increase her dose?

When her doctor told her she wasn't comfortable raising the dose yet, Meghan felt a rush of old, familiar panic. The loss of control brought her straight back to earlier patterns – wanting to restrict, fix, or blame herself. These were survival strategies she'd developed long ago, after an assault in high school had shattered her sense of safety. That trauma had left her with chronic anxiety and a desperate need to control anything she could. The possibility that the GLP-1 might stop working triggered the same fear she'd carried for years: the terror of not being able to rely on someone or something to keep her safe.

Instead of seeing the stall as a possible lull in the medication's effectiveness, Meghan was trapped in a mental loop of her old beliefs that uncertainty meant danger, and if something wasn't working, it must be her fault. Her nervous system couldn't "go with it" because for her, going with it had once meant being unsafe.

The assault had left Meghan deeply traumatized. She blamed herself immediately afterward, and for years she replayed that night in her head, questioning what she wore, how friendly she'd been, or her intuition that hadn't alerted her to impending danger that night. This self-blame became her way of trying to make sense of what she had gone through, an attempt to reclaim control over a moment that had taken all of what felt safe in the world away. But that blame also formed the lens through which she came to see herself and the world.

Keeping the assault a secret left her without the support she needed to process the grief, rage, and confusion. So, she turned inward. Blame, self-doubt and punishment became her coping strategies (the same ones she's using now in her GLP-1 stall). Food became both a comfort and a shield, a buffer from emotional pain and a tool to control the chaos. She also became entangled in cycles of restriction and bingeing, attempting to regain control over a body and life that felt taken from her.

These untrue beliefs hardened over time. Though they created a sense of internal structure that helped her feel safe, they also kept her from fully living. They distorted her relationship with food, intimacy and trust. Especially to herself. She buffered anxiety with food, directed anger inward and struggled deeply to feel safe in close relationships and that life lens would be the same one she tried to problem solve her current GLP-1 medication stall through.

These were Meghan's self-beliefs before the assault:

- Life is safe, fun, and enjoyable.
- It's safe to be vulnerable.
- The world is a safe place.
- Being strong is a valuable asset.
- I can share my spark with the world.
- My family will protect me.

Contrast them with her self-beliefs after the assault:

- Being beautiful is a liability.
- Don't attract attention to your looks, or you may be hurt.
- Life will trick you.
- Nowhere is safe.
- I took everything for granted.
- My family can't protect me.
- I can't depend on anyone for safety.
- No one is going to come save me.
- I need to hide to be safe.

The beliefs she formed went directly against her true nature of being open, kind, outgoing, gregarious, fun, and vibrant. This dissonance created a constant hum of anxiety. She didn't know how to reconcile the two versions of herself. But as we began working together, she slowly began to consider a radical idea: that she had been doing the best she could with what she had. Her belief system was trying to make sense of the chaos. Food had served as protection, soothing the unprocessed pain just beneath the surface.

Emotional eating began as a strategy to survive tragedy, but over time, it kept her stuck in a loop driven by shame and false beliefs that seemed true because they had been in place for so long. Now they came rushing back to help with her GLP-1 dilemma like old friends coming to the rescue. Tools? Yes. Useful? Sort of. Effective? Only when survival was the immediate goal. Now that she was trying to manage bumps (not traumas) in life like her GLP-1 stall, the old untrue belief system would not work as she hoped and self-compassion was just the tool to help find a more effective approach.

Self-compassion is rooted in the question "How would I treat a friend?" Meghan now considered what she would say to a good friend experiencing a similar situation, but this was a foreign concept to her, which was totally understandable. We started with simple exercises like writing a letter to her younger self, offering comfort and understanding. She took her time and didn't push herself to be kind in an inauthentic way.

However, she struggled with the question, "Am I willing to go through the discomfort of bringing untrue beliefs I have into the present so they will be released?" Believing she was at fault for what happened to her, self-compassion seemed not only like the last thing she should consider but also downright unsafe. She feared that this kind of vulnerability would expose her and create an opening for another harmful situation again.

We explored mindfulness techniques, focusing on the present moment and observing her thoughts and feelings without judgment. These practices helped her connect with her inner child and challenge the false beliefs that had taken root. The hardest part, however, was not learning the techniques themselves but committing to carve out time each day to practice them. This daily effort became an act of self-compassion that slowly taught her she was worthy of the same care she would offer a friend.

Meghan had originally come to me for a nutrition solution for her stalled medication. She believed that if she could figure out why it stopped working, she could regain control and with it, a sense of safety. But what we discovered was that the anxiety caused by the medication stall wasn't really about weight. It was about trauma. It was about control. Her fear the GLP-1 medication might fail mirrored the deeper fear she'd carried since the night of the assault, that she couldn't count on anyone or anything to protect her. That it was something she was doing (or not doing) that would cause failure. All of this isn't to say that there are practical ways she could handle a GLP-1 stall like looking at her protein intake, trying intermittent fasting and getting enough sleep. But remember, practical solutions are not the same as emotional safety and she was getting those two things confused because of the trauma she'd experienced. Like many of us, she was trying to solve her anxiety issue with tools that weren't powerful enough.

This distinction matters. Too often, we treat emotional symptoms with logic. But the mind doesn't hold the wound, the heart does. For healing to happen we must meet those wounds where the live. That's why self-compassion is such a powerful tool.

I asked Meghan to take the risk and approach her hurting parts with tenderness instead of stern course correction. For years, she had avoided her pain with food. But now, she was curious. What if those painful emotions were built on untrue assumptions?

We began her self-compassion journey with a small step. I had her role-play with a loving heart how she might guide a good friend to be less judgmental of herself. Then I had her practice not judging herself when words of criticism arose in her daily life. Meghan's practice of self-compassion was not intended to treat the emotional eating or even her anxiety—it was designed to treat the judgments she formed after going through a big challenge and the resultant feelings that eating helped dampen.

Meghan's biggest challenge was to trust herself enough to walk toward the part of herself that was hurting so she could comfort and soothe it with self-compassion. She took her time and went at her own pace, but she was able to trust in herself and practiced with an open heart. She was able to soothe her judgments and feel the safety of her deep care. When she was able to do that for herself, she was able to navigate her GLP-1 stall with patience, calm and care.

What's Your Level of Self-Compassion?

Who doesn't love a good quiz? Dr. Kristin Neff has developed a helpful questionnaire for assessing the various ways individuals think, feel, and act in relation to self-compassion. It examines how people typically respond to feelings of inadequacy or distress, as well as their levels of mindfulness, self-kindness, and self-judgment.

This assessment explores whether those who are experiencing emotional pain tend to criticize themselves harshly or offer themselves kindness and understanding. It evaluates how individuals perceive their flaws and shortcomings, ranging from severe self-judgment to acceptance and tolerance. It also examines the degree to which individuals practice mindfulness, observing their experiences with a balanced perspective, especially when facing difficult situations.

Responses are calculated on a five-point scale, ranging from "almost never" to "almost always," allowing for a nuanced understanding of individual differences in self-compassion. There is no charge for taking this quiz, and you may gain self-knowledge and insight. Plus, it's easy! You can take the quiz on Dr. Neff's website: self-compassion.org/self-compassion-test. A shorter version is also available on the *Greater Good Magazine* website: greatergood.berkeley.edu/quizzes/take_quiz/self_compassion. Give it a try!

Next are a pair of exercises I use with my clients, which can help deepen what this quiz uncovered for you.

Exercise: Tapping into Your Compassionate Voice

Think of a time when you were upset with yourself or felt that you messed up in some way, perhaps something you did that now makes you cringe when you think about it. Or consider a time when you were facing a big loss, like a layoff or the death of a pet. What did the people around you say? Did they offer words of encouragement and kindness? How often do you say similar things to yourself? Take a minute to consider this: How different is the support and kindness of nice people around you from what you say to yourself?

Now consider how you judge yourself around food and eating. You may have replayed a scene from when you or others didn't see you in the best light. Over and over again, you may have thought about how you handled it.

- "If I had been stronger, I wouldn't have eaten like that."
- "Anyone who heard me say that must have thought I was an idiot."
- "I always say the worst things at the worst moments."
- "Why do I do that? I can't believe I said that; something must be wrong with me."
- "If I had done something differently, I would not feel so bad now."

We usually berate ourselves rather than let ourselves off the hook with kindness. Here is what a self-compassionate voice using the formula above might sound like:

I'm willing to lean in and think about when I said or did something I wish I hadn't. Instead of being hard on myself, I imagine what a kind and loving friend would say to me: "We all have moments when we say something or do something we wish we hadn't! Instead of beating yourself up, could you let yourself off the hook on this one? Yes, it's hard when we say something we wish we hadn't, but what can you give yourself right now to help you feel supported in your upset and even extend kindness toward yourself?"

Exercise: Feeling Self-Compassion in Your Body

1. Take a few centering breaths. Imagine your breath flowing to all parts of your body, and focus on your physical heart and where it sits in your chest.

2. Imagine now that around your physical heart is your compassionate heart. Where is yours located? Focus on that space for a moment and consider that your compassionate heart space is one of the most active places in your body. It's in your body, but more than your body too. It's where love flows in and out of you. What does it feel like? Warm? Soft? Soothing? Comforting?

3. Now imagine you have just experienced a challenge of some kind while being on a GLP-1 medication. Think about one that has stood out from the last few months. What did that feel like? What feelings flooded your body with that challenge?

4. If you had a very caring, loving, and supportive person with you when you had that challenge, what do you think they would say to you?

5. How would you feel hearing and receiving words of encouragement?

6. What does it feel like in your body to be supported with kindness? Take a moment to pause and consider how different it may be than what you are used to.

* * *

Self-compassion has become well known in the healing world in the last decade. That's good news because the world needs it. But often it's added as a side note or afterthought, not as a complete path. It's also often harder to practice than it seems—and I want to take a moment to honor that. Self-compassion takes *practice*, but I promise it's worth the effort. It's not the default most of us resort to when things get hard. Expect that and choose it anyway. We're so hard on ourselves that we'll defend (often to the death) untrue things we believe about ourselves and will justify treating ourselves unkindly without even knowing we're doing it.

This is a paradox, and it's important to understand and expect as you continue reading this book. Your beliefs will argue with you to remain where you are. Expect that, too, but also counter that argument with compassionate understanding. Here are five questions to keep you engaged with your compassionate heart, so practicing compassionate understanding will be easier:

1. Will I remain open to be more loving to myself?
2. How would I treat a friend?
3. Am I willing to treat myself like I would a friend?
4. Can I locate and spend time in my own compassionate heart space?
5. Am I willing to let go of being right, in order to be loving?

Chapter Takeaways

- Self-compassion consists of self-kindness, common humanity, and mindfulness. It's not the same as empathy or self-esteem.
- It's evidence-based and effective for a multitude of psychological issues, including body image and any type of disordered eating.
- It can help us break the cycle of shame and self-blame that often accompany food struggles.
- It's easy to learn but not easy to do and requires practice and patience.
- It often feels completely unnatural to practice self-compassion, and you may experience uncomfortable feelings.
- To practice self-compassion, ask yourself, "How would I treat a friend?"
- Practicing self-compassion lights up the reward centers of the brain—the same places in the brain that light up during emotional eating.

Chapter 5

Get to Know Your Inner Eater

"Dig here," the angel said—"in your soul, in your soul."
—St. John of the Cross

Each of us has an Inner Eater. It's the part inside that makes decisions about food, manages our relationship with it, and sustains the fundamental beliefs we hold about food and ourselves in relation to it. Guided by the aggregated experiences of life, our Inner Eater might say something practical, such as, "I don't usually feel well after I eat this, so I'm not going to." Alternatively, it could offer an unsolicited and incorrect opinion, such as, "You don't deserve that dessert." Some call this intuition, but it's more than that. It's a rule book for eating that's used every single time we think about eating and with every bite that passes our lips.

GLP-1 medications offer a unique window of opportunity: With the physical hunger and food thoughts temporarily quieted, you can finally hear and examine this Inner Eater's voice with clarity. This provides the perfect chance to identify and rewrite the rules that have been silently guiding your eating for years.

In this chapter, we'll explore the Inner Eater and its rule book. You'll understand why the rules are there and learn how to use your heart to change them (if you'd like).

How the Inner Eater Is Formed

We're all born with a simple on/off switch when it comes to food: We're either hungry or not, and we react accordingly. Most newborns cry or make noise to indicate hunger and then simply quiet themselves or fall asleep when satiated. There are no decisions or questions or second guesses or rules that guide behavior. They operate reflexively based on an innate need and respond automatically when that need is met.

As life unfolds, that simple on/off switch morphs into a wall of buttons, dials, flashing lights, levers, knobs, and alarms. There's nothing reflexive or simple about it any longer; every bite becomes a series of decisions, emotions, considerations, judgments, talking points, counterpoints, pros, and cons. Standing in front of this wall is your Inner Eater—the part of you that decides how to eat, when to eat, why to eat, and what to eat, along with any and all "rules" about food and eating. Shaped by a complex web of personal history and perspectives, experiences and emotions, decisions about fairness and life, and feelings of comfort and safety, your Inner Eater translates "What do I believe?" into "How, when, why, and what do I eat?"

For example, a parent's benign statement, "No dessert unless you've finished everything on your plate," can begin informing your Inner Eater. So too can observations of those around you, such as hearing a parent comment on their spouse's weight or watching "the fat kid" at school getting picked last for the team. More direct inputs are also common contributors to your Inner Eater, such as hearing your grandmother tell you that you'll surely find a spouse/partner once you lose some weight or having a classmate say that the only reason you were invited to a party was because you were pretty.

By capturing and remembering these many signals and inputs, your Inner Eater gets rooted in the decisions you've made—correctly or incorrectly—about yourself, your world, your friendships, your family, and your expectations, rather than adapting to the ongoing messiness of life. This rootedness locks you and your Inner Eater in a time and place of relative emotional immaturity and fragility, guiding your relationship with food for years to come.

Imagine an eight-year-old girl bullied at school because of her weight, who decides in that moment that she is unlovable. Consequently, she believes that losing weight is the only way to be loved—a belief developed to cope with an incredibly painful situation and taken as truth by her Inner Eater, influencing how she eats for decades. Now, imagine this same girl at thirty-three years old, being asked to create a "healthy mindset" around food or to start down the path of intuitive eating. Her childhood beliefs will likely prove to be an obstacle she can't easily overcome, because they have consciously and unconsciously become the foundation of her relationship with food.

Some examples of what your Inner Eater might say include the following:

- "Pain? Food will help."
- "Ultra-processed foods are not good for me."
- "If I ever go off my GLP-1 medication, I'll definitely gain that weight back."
- "If I believe that weight loss is good, I'm following diet culture."
- "I know I'm worthless, so who cares if I eat the whole pizza?"
- "I lost all that weight; now I'm an impostor. I'm really a fat person in a thin body."
- "A low-carbohydrate diet is essential."
- "Stop eating that right now, you horrible person."
- "Bread is very bad for me."
- "I can only eat 1,200 calories today, or I'll gain weight."
- "There's only one safe way for me to eat."
- "One wrong bite means that I'm a failure."

What the Inner Eater believes is based on what it has heard or learned, and it will inform the core of your belief system around food and execute those beliefs. Ultimately, the Inner Eater is doing its best to keep you safe and minimize discomfort at all costs. But what the Inner Eater doesn't tell you is that it may not be—and usually isn't—operating on current information. The good news is that self-compassion is an extremely effective way to examine what the Inner Eater believes and why and to update those beliefs to match your current goals and wishes.

How the Inner Eater Gets Shaped over Time

Sometimes, these beliefs are obvious, such as when someone has celiac disease and therefore avoids gluten, or when a person feels strongly about animal rights and chooses to be vegan. However, some beliefs are less visible, and we may not realize their significant influence over how and why we eat the way we do. The belief systems of the Inner Eater are tied to each person's emotional development—the nurturing and safety they did or did not receive. It's important to remember that emotional maturity and resilience can vary significantly in different areas of someone's life.

For example, a highly intelligent person with three college degrees and a multimillion-dollar business may exhibit a low level of emotional maturity in certain areas of their life due to a lack of emotional nurturing from their caregivers. Outwardly, they may appear very successful, but inwardly they may feel like an impostor, believe it's not safe to trust anyone, and feel unworthy of a fulfilling life. Their Inner Eater will compensate for these negative self-beliefs through their relationship with food, until they decide to view themselves differently.

This is why we see such variance among highly successful people who struggle privately with food issues. A tech executive who seems to "have it all" might be struggling with binge eating. Moreover, when a stressful life event occurs, such as a breakup or a lawsuit from a business partner, they will react with food at the emotional maturity level of their Inner Eater, which often exhibits maladaptive coping skills. This is also why so many people struggle with intuitive eating and mindset challenges—their nervous system's operation is based on flawed data about their own worth because that's what they were taught.

The more false beliefs your Inner Eater holds about you (or the more Life Jackets it wears), the harder it becomes for you to distinguish between practical and existential choices. This also makes it easier for your Inner Eater to become dysregulated when faced with a challenge.

While it's true that the Inner Eater is doing its best with what it has, it often harbors shame. Remember, shame is a toxic belief that shifts from "I did something wrong" to "I am wrong." *An Inner Eater burdened with shame will create an action plan around food to compensate for this perceived deficit.* Instead of focusing on building your brilliance and fostering love from a place of abundance, an Inner Eater filled with shame will focus on compensating and fixing shame-based beliefs, which stem from a place of lack. A few examples of this would be Inner Eaters that believe it's best to skip breakfast to "save calories," strict eating schedules, extreme restriction like only eating 800 calories a day or even eliminating entire food groups.

With this input and all its inherent biases, your Inner Eater often acts by creating strict rules about the "right" and "wrong" ways to eat to protect you from pain, loss, hurt, chaos, illness, disease, and even death. The Inner Eater takes these experiences and shapes our relationship with food through rules, many of which keep us in a cycle of shame.

Rules like "if you were really focused on being healthy, you wouldn't eat junk food" or "people who cared about themselves wouldn't snack at night or go back for seconds at dinner."

Exercise: How Does Your Inner Eater Feel Right Now?

Take a centering breath and close your eyes. Imagine that your Inner Eater is sitting beside you. If you were to "lean in" to any discomfort your Inner Eater has right now, could you describe it? What does it feel like? Sound like? Be as descriptive as you can and add anything in that seems appropriate to describe this discomfort. Answer the following questions:

- How often are you aware of what your Inner Eater is experiencing?
- How does it feel to be aware of your Inner Eater?
- Is it challenging to lean in to notice what your Inner Eater feels like?

Danni's Story

Danni was a client of mine who did this exercise. She had gone off her GLP-1 medication because she had reached her health and weight goals. But, shortly after stopping the medication, her food noise and cravings came back and she gained 10 pounds. She thought all her food issues were gone but now was questioning the path forward and was worried. I suggested she check in with her Inner Eater to understand more clearly what she was feeling and what she was afraid of, along with any old beliefs that may still be lurking that affected how she ate and saw herself in this new place.

After centering herself, taking a few calming breaths and visualizing her Inner Eater, I asked Danni if she could see her Inner Eater if she used her imagination. Danni started tearing up and shared that her Inner Eater was full of rage, wanting to lash out at anyone who came near. Crouched in a corner, holding a battle axe she screamed at Danni to get away. I asked Danni how she felt to be aware of the scene she was witnessing, and Danni said she was scared to go closer for fear that her Inner Eater was going to harm her. I asked if she could tell what her Inner Eater was experiencing and she paused for a moment and shared that her Inner Eater said, "I'm not going down without a fight. You can't give me peace with food and my body and just take it all away. I am preparing for battle." By doing this exercise and taking the time to visualize her Inner Eater, Danni realized that what she was witnessing wasn't simple aggression, but a protective response to betrayal. "I see now that my Inner Eater isn't attacking me, Danni reflected. "She's defending herself because she trusted the GLP-1 medication had solved our problems with food. When the challenges returned, she felt deeply deceived." Danni recognized that beneath the rage was profound disappointment. Her Inner Eater had experienced the medication as creating a false hope and now would refuse to be vulnerable again, echoing a similar pattern from growing up having an alcoholic father who would get sober and often relapse. Together, we talked about this, and I explained that her Inner Eater was trying to protect her from more pain, and she could rebuild trust with this hurting part of herself.

Not Every Inner Eater Is the Same
Everyone's Inner Eater is different, so how they handle a challenge is dictated by the level of emotional resilience (or lack of resilience) they have. Resilience is the ability to manage and recover from hard experiences, and highly traumatized individuals have poorly regulated Inner Eaters. I think it's important to contrast how regulated and dysregulated Inner Eaters respond to a challenge.

Here's an example: Lori, who has just been laid off from her job, is terrified, mad, and confused. Below are two ways that her Inner Eater might respond to challenging circumstances.

Example 1: The Dysregulated Inner Eater
If Lori has a dysregulated Inner Eater, she believes she is undeserving of happiness—a byproduct of a mentally abusive upbringing. This belief leads her to restrict her food intake, which paradoxically calms her because it reinforces her unconscious belief of unworthiness. After being laid off, Lori immediately enters a cycle of starving and bingeing to cope with the stress of finding a new job. The bingeing temporarily helps manage the stress, while the starving punishes her perceived inadequacies, which she believes to be the reason for her layoff, and soothes the mental chatter labeling her a failure.

Example 2: The Regulated Inner Eater
If Lori's Inner Eater is regulated, she accepts that life can be hard and that dysregulated behaviors are sometimes part of it. She doesn't judge herself for occasionally engaging in such behaviors and knows she has

other tools she can use to face life's challenges. After her layoff, she allows herself to fully experience her feelings of terror, anger, and confusion. She devises a care plan to process these emotions, regularly checking in with herself to assess her needs.

Lori practices self-kindness, reassuring herself with affirmations like "This is hard, scary, and confusing, but you're going to be okay. You didn't do anything wrong." She challenges her self-critical thoughts, forgiving herself with statements like "I forgive myself for believing I'm a failure because I got laid off." While food cravings are part of this process, she acknowledges and forgives these impulses, saying, "I forgive myself for believing that food is the best way to deal with this discomfort and pain."

This work is uncomfortable, and at times her Inner Eater suggests that bingeing would ease everything. In the past, she would have tried to suppress these urges. Now, she welcomes them with simple breathing exercises and asks what the voice needs to feel safe, discovering that it often craves comfort and connection.

Exercise: What Does Your Inner Eater Believe?

As Lori's story demonstrates, we can't change what happened to us, but we can change what we decide about ourselves, and this applies to what the Inner Eater decides as well. Let's take some time to discover what your Inner Eater believes, and why. Ask yourself the following questions:

- What role has my Inner Eater played in my life?
- What does my Inner Eater believe about the role of food in my life?
- What does my Inner Eater believe about my worth and value?
- What has happened to my Inner Eater over the course of my life so far?
- What does my Inner Eater want or need from me?

Here's an example of common answers:

- My Inner eater plays the role of the all-knowing fierce protector.
- My Inner Eater believes the role of food in my life to be the one source of enjoyment I was never allowed growing up.
- My Inner Eater believes that I have less value than others and have to prove my worth.
- My Inner Eater has been on duty 24 hours a day since I can remember. It's been challenged, forgotten, and treated poorly, yet doing the best it can.

- My Inner Eater wants to be acknowledged, listened to, cared for, and really wants extra help, so it doesn't feel alone and solely responsible.

Asking these questions can strengthen the communication you have with your Inner Eater. The more communication you have with your Inner Eater, the easier it will be to find out what happened to it, what it believes, and what it needs from you.

Most of us are not consciously connected to our Inner Eater, even though it unconsciously drives much of our relationship with food. The more curious and open-minded we are about the role of our Inner Eater and the more we practice asking these questions, the more we can bring to light insights about how our Inner Eater has thoughts and behaviors around food that are outdated and incorrect—and the more readily we can change them. For example, my Inner Eater learned at nine years old that fat girls are never in the popular group at school. This belief set a precedent for my entire relationship with food, one that persisted until I decided to change it. Growing up in Florida, where I was constantly in a bathing suit, I was called fat and ugly. My nine-year old self thought that fat and ugly girls weren't invited to birthday parties. They weren't part of the "cool girls" social group; all things I wanted at nine. To stop being called fat and ugly, my relationship with food had to change. Food became the enemy so that I could stop eating it and therefore stop *being* fat to stop being *called* fat and become more socially accepted.

We say that we grow and learn and mature and, yes, that happens. But, if you ask me today what it felt like to be called fat and ugly at nine years old, I can recall with lightning speed what that was like and how it impacted how I saw myself in the world. It's not that today I don't still feel the sting of that, because I do. If someone called me fat today, I'd be bothered. But what's different today is that I know how to care for myself when I hear horrible things. I know how to give myself the inner safety and not turn on myself and go into a shame spiral (remember that shame keeps emotional growth locked so we can't grow). I know how to care for myself hurting from mean things people say. I know how to give myself space to feel dysregulated and tender.

When you address your relationship with your Inner Eater and remove all judgments about yourself, the following three things will happen:

1. Your Inner Eater won't need to get your attention for love and care, so it won't be as present.
2. You won't be as affected whether you emotionally eat or not.
3. You will increase your emotional resilience, better preparing you for life's ups and downs.

Cara's Story

Cara came to me wanting to start a cleanse and needed help with her emotional attachment to food. Her naturopathic doctor had recommended a four-week food protocol to help with digestion and energy, which included the temporary removal of some foods. Cara had completed the program before and loved the results, especially the weight loss and energy boost. She felt amazing while eating the prescribed fruits and vegetables, but each time she finished the protocol, she reverted back to her emotional eating patterns, which included binge eating unhealthy foods. She felt powerless to resist food and wondered if she had a food addiction.

What made her situation particularly complex was that Cara had recently completed a maintenance phase after being on a GLP-1 medication. The medication had helped her manage appetite and lose weight, but after discontinuing it, her food cravings surged again. She was frustrated and confused – why, after all her efforts and progress, was she back in the same cycle?

As we began discussing her relationship with food, Cara became emotional. She admitted that eating filled a deep void inside her, one she couldn't quite explain. When I gently asked what that void might be, she paused and said "I don't like myself." For Cara, emotional eating was not just about food. It was to cope with a painful belief about her worth. She had been trying to fix this hole with cleanses, lifestyle changes, and medications, but none of these efforts addressed the deeper wound: her self-dislike.

Cara had never considered that approaching her inner pain with compassion might improve, and even heal, her relationship with food. Compassion toward herself felt counterintuitive and challenging, but our conversation stirred something in her. She became open to trying a new way. Together, we created a simple daily practice of inward reflection to help begin connecting with her Inner Eater. She understood that emotional eating would continue until she addressed the belief at the root of her self-judgment.

I asked her if she remembered when she first decided she didn't like herself. She nodded. Cara shared that although her family lived in a wealthy suburb, they struggled financially. In an effort to fit in with her affluent peers, she began shoplifting so she could look like everyone else. One day, she was caught and arrested. That moment changed everything. It left her with deep shame, humiliation, and anger toward herself. She had never told anyone about this and the memory had been locked away, sitting quietly in the corner of her mind, protected by her Inner Eater. She had never forgiven herself for what happened. Her Inner Eater had taken on the pain and carried it.

While on the cleanse, I suggested she practice the Inner Eater Meditation to start building a relationship with this part of herself. Each day, she was to visualize and connect with her Inner Eater, gently acknowledging its presence and opening a dialogue. The goal was to continue this practice until her intense feelings around food began to soften and she gained the lived experience and confidence to believe that the safety she was searching for wasn't in food – it was within her.

Through this practice, Cara discovered that her Inner Eater was a part of herself that was longing for care, understanding and forgiveness. She learned that this part of her had been trying to protect her from difficult emotions by using food as comfort. Her Inner Eater believed it wasn't safe for her secret to come out, because shoplifting seemed like proof she was a bad person. But when she approached this part with curiosity and compassion, recognizing that she had simply been a young girl trying to make friends, something shifted. When she acknowledged how she and her Inner Eater had held this secret together and how the comfort of eating was one of the only tools they had – it allowed that protective energy to begin to relax. Her Inner Eater realized the belief it held could change. She no longer felt the urgency to use food to compensate or control.

As Cara built a relationship with her Inner Eater, she began to develop emotional strategies beyond willpower or medication to manage her eating patterns.

Over time, this practice transformed her relationship with food. Not because it swept all her issues away, but because she learned to become attuned to her body's actual hunger signals and emotional needs. She learned how to be present with herself. She practiced self-kindness instead of judgment. She felt more resilient, more confident, and more capable, especially after healing the core belief she wasn't worthy of love and care. The most powerful shift she experienced came not from something she took, but from the care she offered to herself.

This inner work also became a turning point in her GLP-1 journey. While the medication had effectively reduced her appetite, it had not addressed the emotional roots of her eating. After she stopped taking it, the cravings returned. But now, instead of panicking or blaming herself, she had a relationship with the part of her that once turned to food. Her Inner Eater no longer had to act out in secret or protect an old wound alone. For the first time, she felt like had something more sustainable than medicine: self-trust. Her relationship with food was no longer about control, but about connection.

Exercise: "Meeting Your Inner Eater" Meditation

This is a meditation exercise to meet your Inner Eater, so that you can understand what it believes and give it what it needs to feel safe through reparenting and self-compassion. This improves your relationship with food. When you are curious and caring about your Inner Eater, you regulate your nervous system, increase your emotional resilience, and change what it believes. That means you are nurturing your Inner Eater to operate in the current time and most likely with an updated set of skills for goals you have for yourself. (This meditation is available for you to listen to at Insight Timer: insighttimer.com/thelovingdiet/ guided-meditations/the-inner-eater-meditation.)

- While this meditation exercise only takes about 10-15 minutes, be sure to allow yourself enough time and a quiet, safe space.
- Know that the Inner Eater might be different every time you visit it, and it may or may not be static in time, so any age or issue could present itself when you meet it.
- You have all the tools inside of you at this moment that the Inner Eater needs to feel safe, comforted, and connected. Engage your imagination at any time to help in this exercise.
- Emotional discomfort or sadness may arise because of this exercise. If that happens, allow the feelings to surface and take care of yourself

by nurturing yourself. This could be making your favorite tea, calling a friend, getting into a warm bath, or taking a walk. This will help complete the life cycle of the emotion you are experiencing that the Inner Eater has been holding frozen in time.

Let's begin:

Close your eyes and find a comfortable position to complete this meditation. Set the intention that you are going to meet and visit with your Inner Eater, only doing what feels comfortable.

Take a few deep breaths and focus on relaxing your body, allowing your breath to travel anywhere it might be holding stress.

Place your awareness on your physical heart and notice how it works all by itself pumping blood to all parts of your body.

Now place your awareness on your compassionate heart—a place near your physical heart but the place where compassion is generated inside of you and the place where love and compassion flows in and out of you.

Imagine yourself standing inside your compassionate heart and seeing a door. Imagine walking through that door into a hallway.

As you walk down the hallway, see another door at the end. This door is going to take you into a room where you can visit your Inner Eater. This is a peaceful, calm room—a gentle meeting place, if you will. Remember, there is no right or wrong way to meet with your Inner Eater.

Open the door and walk into the room. What do you notice? What do you see? Take a moment to take in where you are.

Locate where in this room your Inner Eater is and walk over to it. What does it look like? How old is it? What is it wearing? How does it feel?

Take a few deep breaths and allow all this to sink in; be aware of what you are experiencing. Trust whatever comes forward from you and your Inner Eater. You are there simply to gather information and meet a part of yourself that has a pretty big job.

Tell your Inner Eater: "I have come to visit you because I'm very curious about what you believe and what has happened to you."

Wait for its response. Take your time with this. Notice whatever it shares with you as openly as you can.

Then tell your Inner Eater, "Thank you so much for sharing this with me. I'm so sorry this happened to you. You haven't done anything wrong."

Wait to see how it responds to you. Notice what you both are experiencing.

Ask your Inner Eater if it needs anything from you or if there is anything you can give it right now. Repeat, "I'm so sorry this has been hard. Can you tell me more about what happened to you?" Wait for any response with genuine curiosity.

Remember to come back to your breath if you are feeling a lot of emotion.

Wait for its response and, if you are able, give it what it needs. Remember, in this place you can manifest anything you need to give to your Inner Eater, like a hug. Or if it was scary to be with, gently congratulate yourself for the courage to meet it. Again, notice what you both are experiencing as you are being heard and seen.

If your Inner Eater asks to be let out or to come with you, consider this option. Your Inner Eater may just want to share its experience with you and stay where it's at. If your Inner Eater was silent, and all you could pick up on was feelings and colors, that's okay too.

Thank the Inner Eater for letting you visit. If you want, let it know that you will be back or invite it out with you to come live with you now. Do only what feels right for you.

See yourself now walking out of that room (with or without your Inner Eater) and making your way back down the hallway into the compassionate heart space you started in. Take a breath and see your physical heart now. If your Inner Eater has come back with you, see it sitting next to you. Give it anything it may need. Allow yourself to adjust coming back into your body, wiggling your fingers and toes and fluttering your eyelids. Take a moment before getting up and recording what you can of your experience in your journal.

* * *

Getting to know your Inner Eater is a journey worth taking. This inner part manages your relationship with food based on beliefs it formed to keep you safe. While these beliefs may no longer be true or accurate, you can update them with the power of your heart and inner kindness. Most of us have spent years at the mercy of our Inner Eater's rules, unaware that these outdated beliefs still dictate our eating decisions. By approaching our Inner Eater with curiosity, kindness, and understanding rather than rules, force, and logic, we can transform its operating system from one focused on safety to one rooted in compassion and self-awareness.

Chapter Takeaways
- You, like everyone, have an Inner Eater that has a set of beliefs that translate into your relationship with food.
- Examining what your Inner Eater believes is very helpful for your post-GLP-1 life, so you can clear up any untrue beliefs, which can improve your relationship with food and body.
- Your Inner Eater has created beliefs, rules, laws, superstitions, and structure meant to take care of you in some way.
- Many of the beliefs the Inner Eater has are not factual and are based on inaccurate information used to assess your emotional safety.
- Your Inner Eater has a level of emotional intelligence it operates on based on how it was nurtured growing up. When stressful life events happen, it may exhibit dysregulated behaviors, especially around food.
- You can discover what your Inner Eater believes by leaning in toward its hurt parts with curiosity and learning how to listen to it.
- You can change what the Inner Eater believes by giving it the compassion, kindness, and connection it never had before.
- When you do this, your Inner Eater will create a new relationship with food based on the updated view of yourself.
- You can practice the "Meeting Your Inner Eater" meditation to understand what the Inner Eater believes, as well as why and how you can create a safe, meaningful connection with it, so it can form beliefs that are built on safety and abundance, not lack.

Chapter 6

The Emotional Math of Eating

Only love can truly save the world.
—Wonder Woman

There's a belief in our culture that the amount of time we spend thinking about food is inversely correlated to the health of our relationship with it—that the less (or more) we think about food the better (or worse) our relationship with it truly is. At the same time, negative thoughts about food are considered "bad," and positive thoughts about it are "good." This is a simplistic and inaccurate framing of the issue. What truly matters is breaking free of the judgments we have about our food-related thoughts, regardless of how much or how little we think about food and what those thoughts are. Being on a GLP-1 medication often dampens the biochemical signals your brain produces, making it easier to tell the difference between true hunger and non-true hunger like emotional eating.

In this chapter, we'll delve into how much you think about food and why the frequency of these thoughts doesn't necessarily indicate a problem. I'll introduce you to the concept of the emotional math of eating—the internal weighing and measuring we apply to each bite—and we'll explore how developing self-compassionate approaches toward your thoughts can provide relief and pave the way for lasting change and peace. That way, if you eventually stop taking a GLP-1 medication, you'll be able to tackle the emotional math equation. Additionally, I'll guide you through a process to increase compassion-based mindfulness skills that will help dissolve underlying judgments around food.

Thinking About Food Takes Up a Lot of Time

One of the first questions I ask new students and clients I work with is this: How much time do you spend thinking about food each day? If you're on a GLP-1 medication, you may clearly remember how much you *used to think about food* and be enjoying how much you don't think about food now, so if you are, think back to how much of your day was spent thinking about food before. Often I hear the answer "A LOT—most waking hours and some sleeping ones too." Yet few people are willing to say the quiet thing out loud to themselves, let alone a relative stranger. After all, admitting that 75 percent of your daily thoughts are about food feels like confessing to failure right from the start.

Clients have explained that it's like a constant stream of negative mental chatter. And the number one wish I hear from them is this: that they wouldn't think about food so much, because they're certain that if they just didn't think about food, their lives would be easier, and they would feel lighter and freer. If you're not experiencing food noise like you used to as you read this, it's important to know that it's the medication that's driving that, and if you ever come off the medication, it will most likely return, so this is an important topic to cover with you.

The wish everyone has is to simply banish their thoughts about food, either by eliminating them altogether or replacing them with words of encouragement and positivity. The hope and expectation are that doing so would free them from the exhaustion and bring about peace. However, attempts to overpower any kind of thinking—especially when that thinking is focused on safety and outcomes—require immense energy and are often unsuccessful.

Let's consider a different approach: cultivating self-compassion toward our thoughts. This activates the reward centers of the brain, offering relief from the very thoughts that consume and exhaust us. It creates distance between us and the judgment that our thinking is bad. Additionally, it provides a new focus, which can help reduce overthinking about food.

So, are we trying to change our thinking? In a way, yes. But not from a place of wrongness, willpower, or unhealthy pressure. We're going to appreciate that our thinking is doing its best for us. Through self-compassion, we can change our thinking by entering through the back door of kindness and appreciation, recognizing that we're doing the best we can, rather than trying to break down the front door through sheer willpower.

Is It a Whisper or a Scream?

Some thinking about food is practical and necessary—for sheer survival, meal planning, shopping, dietary/health considerations, and following recipes, among other reasons. What we're focusing on here is all the thinking done *outside* of the practical and necessary that touches on the more sensitive and loaded aspects often associated with food.

Let's take a very simple question that any of us might encounter: Should I have oatmeal or a smoothie for breakfast? While some of us might answer very practically—oatmeal, because it's faster to make and clean up, and I only have ten minutes—many others answer the question with even more questions, thoughts, and observations that instantaneously devolve into a tangled mess of internal chaos:

- I love the taste of oatmeal, but will it make me feel bloated?
- If I choose a smoothie, I might feel less bloated later, but will it fill me up?
- I love adding blueberries to my oatmeal.
- My new vegan protein is chalky, but it's 100 fewer calories than my normal oatmeal breakfast with maple syrup and butter.
- I enjoy my smoothies with peanut butter, but what about the calories?
- Why do I think about this so much?
- If I eat too much now, I'll have to use less salad dressing tonight.
- Why can some people eat whatever they want, but I can't?
- What would life be like if I didn't have to think about food?
- Should I have a smoothie to increase my protein?
- Does oatmeal have too many carbs?

I refer to this internal weighing, measurement, evaluation, and food analysis as the "emotional math of eating." For some, it's intermittent and barely a whisper; for others, it's a constant screaming presence at every snack and meal. Regardless, the internal process is always the same: a seemingly endless loop of thinking, questioning, doubt, fear, and concern, all tied to decoding the cost/benefit, guilt/pleasure, and pain/joy of food.

The Emotional Math of Frozen Yogurt

During the early stages of the Covid-19 pandemic, all restaurants in my area shut down. As a result, grocery shopping, prepping, cooking, and dishes for my family of six nearly did me in, even though my husband was helpful. Getting our four teenagers to put their dishes in the dishwasher or pick up a sponge to clean a counter was an almost daily battle for me. Preparing for and cleaning up after three meals a day was a big personal challenge I didn't handle well.

One day, out of frustration about the lack of help I was receiving in the kitchen, I screamed at our kids and threw a plate on the floor that shattered. I declared I was going on a mothering strike and stomped out of the room to watch 12 straight hours of Netflix alone.

During those stressful weeks, my thoughts about the first thing I'd do when the world opened back up were always about food—specifically frozen yogurt from a restaurant in San Francisco that makes it from scratch and tops it with fancy olive oil and salt. It was going to be my reward for all the cooking and cleaning I had done for all those weeks.

When restaurants began opening for takeout, I was filled with anticipation like a kid on Christmas morning. I know I wasn't unique in that regard, but it's possible I was the only person in the Bay Area who wanted this particular frozen yogurt from this particular restaurant. So, when the day arrived and the restaurant started taking orders again, my husband and I made a trip out of it. We brought our beloved pug, Milo, into the city and decided to hike a pretty oceanfront trail before picking up the yogurt. I was absolutely giddy. Finally! The day had come! Yogurt! And no dishes!

But I noticed my anxiety ramped up almost immediately when we started our hike—so much so that my thoughts about food consumed me the entire walk. Being out for the first time in forever wasn't top of mind. Being with my husband and dog wasn't either. And neither was the breathtaking scenery surrounding us. Instead, my brain was focused on yogurt:

- I just want this walk to be over to get my yogurt. I'm so excited!
- I really wish I could eat two yogurts—I'm so hungry.
- It's so nice to be out and enjoying this day.
- Why is everyone I see on this walk so thin? Why was I born with a naturally slow metabolism?
- Do I really want yogurt? I have a dairy sensitivity, so I should probably avoid it.

- If I were strong, I'd say no to the sugar and skip this treat.
- It's been so long since I've been able to order anything at a restaurant. I really missed it!
- Life feels so unfair. I have to work 10 times harder to lose weight than everyone else.
- Everyone on this hike looks so put together. I bet they aren't thinking about food.
- OMG, stop the overthinking! I do this for a living and know how to eat.
- It's not like I've deprived myself during Covid. I've gained weight and been adventurous with food lately. So what?
- Stop fixating on something that isn't even in short supply in your life!
- Why am I thinking about this yogurt so much? Just enjoy the walk. Enjoy your life.
- How much farther do I have on this walk? I just want it to be over. Exercise is such a challenge for me.
- It's not too late to say no to the yogurt.
- Under no circumstances do I want to say no to the yogurt. Life has been so hard for all of us, and rewarding myself with a frozen yogurt is okay...

Finally, in the car outside the restaurant, my husband handed me the yogurt. Exhausted, I looked at him and said, "I need to tell you something that I've been struggling with." I then explained to him what my last 90 minutes had been like and the thinking and overthinking and rethinking and questioning and doubting that I'd experienced—all the back-and-forth, negotiations, and bargaining. I started to tear up.

He gently took my hand halfway through his yogurt and said, "Jessica, I'm so sorry. All that for frozen yogurt? That's so much emotional math to do! How do you even function?"

He couldn't have been more right. That day, I realized that it wasn't the amount of time I devoted to thinking about food. Not at all. It was literally everything else: the judgment I placed on my thinking about food; the value I placed on whether my thoughts were "disordered"; the level of effort I extended to "fixing my thinking"; and the weight of trying to prove how healthy (or unhealthy) I was.

It. Was. Exhausting. Whether I devoted five or five hundred minutes per week to the topic, I was always emotionally spent by the internal computations.

Stop, or Change, Your Thinking

Society at large makes clear what it thinks we should do: Stop thinking about food so much (i.e., do less emotional math) and/or think more "healthy" thoughts to at least neutralize the emotional math we perform around eating. Here are some of the things I've heard from clients and read in articles that aim to minimize, eliminate, or change our internal food computations:

- Just stop thinking about food so much.
- Change your thinking about food to regain control.
- Adopt new food habits that will push out old food habits.
- Stop labeling food as "good" or "bad" to stop thinking about eating "bad" foods.
- Think less by listening to your intuition and the wisdom of your body.
- Heal your trauma, then you won't think about food.
- Eat a low-carb diet to stop your brain from craving sugar all the time.
- Get off social media—it's causing you to overthink.

Sound familiar? If only it were that easy or that effective.

Hundreds of books promise to tame your thoughts by helping you change your mindset, build healthy habits, hack your neurobiology, or learn the importance of sheer willpower. But how do you solve a heart-based problem like emotional eating with mind-based solutions? Even if you could change your mindset about food, and even if you could summon the willpower to not eat the food in the first place, you're still left with the *feelings* of wrongness, inadequacy, and brokenness brought on by food, and these feelings are the fuel of self-judgment.

You are not wrong, and you do not need fixing. This realization alone will vastly improve your relationship with food.

Where Do We Go from Here?

While it's a positive step to acknowledge our thoughts about food, it's not enough to address the root of why our relationship with food and our body is challenging. These thoughts are fueled by deeply held beliefs, and focusing solely on the thoughts themselves is like treating the symptoms without addressing the underlying cause. Mind-based solutions alone can't fully resolve a heart-centered issue like emotional eating.

Instead, let's explore how harnessing self-kindness and mindfulness can release judgments about our thoughts and feelings around food. This shift in focus can cultivate a healthier relationship with both our minds and our meals.

I experienced this shift firsthand. By stopping my attempts to change my thinking and instead focusing on being kind and supportive to myself, regardless of my thoughts, I found a new sense of freedom. While my mind was still preoccupied with food, releasing judgment and the belief that something was wrong with me allowed those thoughts to lose their power. I stopped caring if I was thinking about food all day—and that in turn helped me think less about food.

Interestingly, thoughts often change in response to shifting core beliefs, practicing self-compassion, and refraining from harsh self-judgment. These are skills we can develop, rather than trying to forcefully change our thinking.

Many people struggle with the loneliness and exhaustion that come with being preoccupied with food. They long to "shut off the food noise" and regain control. And, right now yours may be at an all-time low, but it's not because it's healed—it's because you're receiving biochemical help that hopefully you can be on forever, but in case you can't, this approach is very helpful, and practicing how to be mindful about your food thoughts now will help you if you run into trouble in the future.

It's logical to assume that changing our thoughts would bring relief, but I've found this approach rarely works. The real solution lies in adding compassion to observation. By approaching our thoughts about food with gentleness and kindness, we realize that neither our thinking nor we are inherently wrong. This takes practice, but it effectively softens the intensity of food-related thoughts.

Instead of trying to bypass our emotional relationship with food, let's explore the power of simply observing our thoughts without judgment. This compassionate approach can create space for healing and transformation.

While excessive thoughts about food might make us feel flawed, it's important to remember that these thoughts are just thoughts, not reflections of our worth. Paradoxically, the more we allow all food thoughts to surface without judgment, the less power they hold over us.

How to Be Mindful of Your Thoughts About Food

I don't think it's possible or beneficial to try to bypass our emotional math. It's just exhausting. So, what would happen if, instead of trying to change our thinking about food, we just observed our thoughts?

What if we allowed our emotional math to live in a place free of judgment, where its existence doesn't even matter or isn't a sign of emotional health? Suddenly, all its power gets stripped away; there's actually no equation to be solved for, no questions that must be answered, no "rights" or "wrongs." Rather, personal complexities with food could simply be accepted as part of our humanity. And in my case, I don't have to worry if I'm thinking too much about food; instead, I can support the part of myself worried I was thinking too much about food and the part of myself worried I wasn't getting it "right." All our thoughts—whether we classify them as good/bad or healthy/unhealthy—can be an opportunity to deeply care for the parts of ourselves that hold misunderstandings about our goodness.

Each of us can create a caring, loving approach to our thoughts. More than mindful neutrality, we can instead embody "radical kindness"—a heart-fueled space free of judgment from our emotional math. This means accepting or allowing our thoughts, whether "good" or "bad." We don't have to agree with our thoughts, but we can make space for them, become curious about them, and see if they can lead us to care for ourselves in a way we hadn't thought of. We can see this approach as a way to use what feels disruptive or challenging as a tool to remember our innate wholeness. We can compassionately embrace all our thoughts and feelings tied to food and eating instead of bypassing, fixing, or removing them.

Positive Thinking vs. Compassionate Thinking

The allure of positive thinking is undeniable. It promises a life of happiness and success, where challenges are merely stepping stones, and every cloud has a silver lining. According to PositivePsychology. com, positive thinking can manifest as being happy even in challenging circumstances, celebrating others' success, and maintaining a positive vision for the future.

However, "thinking positively" sometimes means turning away from your suffering to be happy. Balancing the different kinds of thinking—positive, negative, and compassionate—requires nuance and skill. It's practical not to overly identify with excessive negative thoughts, but it's equally practical not to overly identify with excessive positive thoughts and turn away from the legitimate pain driving negative thoughts. Yet in our social media–driven world, it's often framed as a one-way street: If you don't choose positivity, you're negative.

Toxic positivity, with its "choose happiness" and "positive vibes only" mantras, can invalidate our genuine emotions and disconnect us from our true selves. While gratitude can be a helpful practice, it differs from blind positivity. Gratitude allows us to acknowledge both the positive and negative aspects of our experiences, fostering a more balanced perspective.

The key difference lies in the starting point: care and kindness. Compassionate thinking doesn't deny the reality of our struggles; instead, it embraces them with understanding and warmth.

Let's consider the difference between positive and compassionate thinking about emotional eating. Here's an example of each:

Positive thinking: "I will use my willpower and simply not think about how challenging my relationship with food (or my body) is."

Compassionate thinking: "I'm having challenging thoughts about my relationship with food (or my body). I acknowledge this struggle and will be kind to myself as I navigate this."

Compassionate thinking involves acknowledging our thoughts and feelings without judgment and offering ourselves the same kindness and support we would offer a friend. This approach allows us to:

- **Stop trying to change our thoughts.** We can't always control what we think, but we can choose how we respond to those thoughts.
- **Acknowledge and allow our thoughts.** By recognizing our thoughts without getting caught up in them, we create space for them to pass without causing distress.

- **Send kindness toward ourselves.** We can soothe and comfort ourselves when facing difficult thoughts, reminding ourselves that we are worthy of love and support.

This compassionate approach can lead to profound shifts in our relationship with ourselves and our challenges. Instead of battling our thoughts, we learn to befriend them. Here are some examples of compassionate self-talk:

- "As my body changes, I sometimes wonder 'who will I be when I reach my goal weight?' This identity shift is natural and I can approach it with curiosity rather than fear."
- "I'm worried about dinner and people commenting on my appearance. I know I'm taking care of my health in a way that works for me, and I don't owe anyone explanations about my personal journey."
- "I feel anxious about dining out with friends. I can acknowledge this discomfort while still allowing myself to enjoy the social connection, which is just as nourishing as the food."
- "My GLP-1 has reduced my physical hunger. These thought patterns developed over years and will take time to evolve—I'm being patient with this process."
- "What if somehow I end up fat again? It's okay to be worried about the future. I'm not going to judge these thoughts and instead normalize them as part of the weight loss journey I'm taking."
- "When I look in the mirror, sometimes I struggle to recognize my changing body. It's okay to need time to reconnect with the new reflection—my worth remains the same regardless of my size."
- "I notice I'm craving a treat despite not feeling hungry. Instead of judgment, I can ask myself with kindness what I'm really seeking."
- "Even as my outer appearance changes, I sometimes feel the same insecurities inside. Healing my relationship with my body is both an outer and inner journey, and I'm honoring both journeys."

Compassionate thinking takes practice, time, and effort to cultivate. It meets us where we are in a supportive way. By embracing compassionate thinking, we allow a larger container to come forward: We don't have to get our thinking "right" or "positive" to experience healing or peace while at the same time understanding the nuance that overly positive or negative thinking can keep us stuck in an unhelpful cycle with food.

Exercise: Compassionate Space for Your Emotional Math of Eating

Appreciating your thoughts around food doesn't mean giving permission for all behaviors, and compassionate awareness toward your food thoughts is best done in a structured way, similar to meditation. In this exercise, I will share straightforward instructions that will help you start this process for yourself.

At the heart of self-compassion is the question, "Is this a loving behavior toward myself?" But let's face it, many of our thoughts aren't kind. Yet there's a pervasive misunderstanding in the wellness world that the quality of our thoughts is an indicator of our inner and outer health.

My frozen yogurt story illustrates how easy it is to overthink while trying to get our thoughts "right" so we can be "healthy." That continual mental loop can be exhausting. Instead of trying to escape this loop, appreciating your thoughts is a simpler way to find relief.

Suppose you're out to dinner with friends, and you want to order fettuccine but feel that you shouldn't because it isn't "the healthy choice" (or for multiple other reasons) and should instead get the grilled fish and vegetables. This is a great example of something that might set your thinking into overdrive. You may experience a ticker tape of thoughts and judgments in this stressful situation, and your emotions may be heightened.

At first, practicing mindfulness in a stressful situation like this may not be easy. It's best to start with some practice sessions in a quiet space.

The NICE Protocol provides a structured approach to help you build awareness and create a compassionate space to transform your relationship with your thoughts. Becoming aware of your thoughts is like developing a new muscle—it requires consistent practice and patience. To begin this practice, find a quiet space where you can sit comfortably. First, access your compassionate heart space by recalling a clear memory of loving something or someone: perhaps a favorite pet, a beloved friend or grandparent, or your first love. This emotional foundation creates the supportive environment needed for this protocol.

The NICE Protocol in Detail:
1. **Notice:** Deliberately observe your thoughts without judgement. Watch them rise as if they were clouds floating in the sky or text bubbles in a cartoon. Simply acknowledge: "I'm having the thought that..."
2. **Include:** Rather than pushing away uncomfortable thoughts about food or your body, include them in your awareness. Visualize these thoughts in bubbles floating across the room, creating helpful distance between you and the thought.
3. **Comfort:** Offer genuine compassion to yourself for having these thoughts. This might sound like: "It makes sense I'm thinking this way given my experiences" or "I'm being really hard on myself right now, and that's tough."
4. **Experience:** Stay present with the entire process and notice how it feels in your body to observe rather than become your thoughts. Experience the spaciousness and freedom that comes with this separation.

The NICE Protocol in Action:
Imagine you've just finished a meal and the thought arises: "I shouldn't have eaten that second helping."
5. **Notice:** "I'm having the thought that I shouldn't have eaten more food."
6. **Include:** Visualize this thought as a bubble floating nearby—present but not consuming you.
7. **Comfort:** "It makes sense I'd worry about portions. I've been conditioned to think this way, and it's not my fault."
8. **Experience:** Feel the difference between being consumed by guilt versus observing the thought with compassion. Notice any physical sensations of relief or relaxation in your body.

Start by practicing with relatively manageable thoughts like judgments about your last meal: "I should have had a smaller portion" or "If I were strong, I would have said no to eating dessert." As you build this skill, you can apply it to increasingly challenging thoughts.

How To Be Mindful Of Your Thoughts

If I were strong, I'd say 'no' to eating

Imagine your thoughts in
a bubble
floating across the room.

Why This Approach Works

Mindfulness creates space *between* your thoughts allowing them to be present in a neutral way rather than a charged way. This separation reduces the emotional impact and frees you from the intense self-judgment. Most important, it helps you experience not being identified with your thoughts, and that gets you closer to the experience of thought neutrality—no longer judging yourself based on thoughts that are temporary.

Once you've gotten the hang of being mindful of your thoughts, you can advance to appreciating the part of you having that thought. This seemingly simple practice builds profound compassion for the parts of yourself that believe these thoughts will keep you safe.

Watching the part
of you thinking
a thought.

Clara's Story

Clara was in her early 50s and had spent the last three decades navigating the exhausting terrain of chronic dieting, emotional labor, and invisible caregiving. She had two adult children, aging parents with increasing medical needs, and a demanding full-time job in education. Like many women her age, she was used to doing everything for everyone and almost nothing for herself.

When her doctor prescribed a GLP-1 medication to support her metabolic health, Clara felt hopeful. For the first time in years, she didn't feel at war with her appetite. The weight she had struggled with for decades began to come off. Her cravings quieted. Her blood sugar stabilized. She finally felt like her body was cooperating.

But several months into the medication, a different kind of discomfort set in.

Clara no longer thought about food all day, but her mind shifted to something else—how to make sure she never went back. She started watching her body with intense scrutiny. She tracked weight fluctuations, worried about long-term side effects, and monitored every shift in how her clothes fit. Even though she was following the recommended lifestyle support—nutrient-dense meals, strength training, better sleep—she lived with a persistent, gnawing fear.

This was Clara's version of emotional math. It wasn't about what she was eating anymore. It was about how to maintain her progress, how to avoid slipping, and how to stay worthy in the body she now inhabited.

At this point, Clara decided to come see me. Beyond the constant calculations about weight and the pressure to never backslide, we uncovered a deeper truth: Clara carried long-standing beliefs that she had never fully examined. She believed she was the problem—weak, undisciplined, and unable to handle stress without control. She thought that if she could just improve herself—be better, be smaller, be more in control—then life wouldn't feel so overwhelming.

"I just need to keep it together," she said. "It doesn't matter why I feel this way. I just don't want to mess everything up."

"Do you want to keep managing the symptoms or find out why the anxiety is there in the first place?" I asked.

She hesitated. "I guess I've never really thought about why. I just assumed this was who I am. But I'm willing to look."

Here are some of the beliefs Clara uncovered:

- Gaining weight would mean she failed herself and others.
- People only respected her now because she looked different.
- If she wasn't hypervigilant, everything she gained would slip away.
- Her worth depended on her discipline and her ability to keep things in control.
- If she softened, everything would fall apart.
- Wanting weight loss to be easy made her lazy.
- She was asking too much of life to be happy and unburdened.
- Going off the GLP-1 medication might mean life she loves could be taken away.
- Being in a larger body had always meant rejection, so staying small meant staying safe.

Clara came to see that her fear wasn't just about weight. It was about worth. The version of herself she was trying to hold onto was the first one she believed others really approved of. But it was also the first time she had felt some approval toward herself.

The NICE Protocol in Action

To help her interrupt these spiraling thought patterns, I introduced Clara to the NICE Protocol. She agreed to practice it every morning before breakfast, with a journal nearby.

Notice: She began by gently observing her thoughts without believing or resisting them.

"I'm having the thought that if I gain even five pounds, I'll lose everything."

"I'm having the thought that I'm only lovable in this smaller body."

Include: She imagined each thought as a floating text bubble. Present, but not definitive.

"This belief about needing to stay small to stay safe is here today."

Comfort: She placed a hand on her chest and offered herself warmth.

"It makes sense I feel afraid. I've carried this fear for years. Anyone who worked this hard to feel seen would feel nervous to lose it."

Experience: She let herself feel the anxiety in her body—the tight chest, shallow breath, urge to control. Instead of reacting, she stayed with it. Her breath slowed. Her tension softened. The panic began to pass.

Meeting her Inner Eater

Though Clara's Inner Eater no longer pushed her toward food, it hadn't disappeared. It had simply shifted. Now, it carried decades of shame and fear—of becoming invisible again, of being judged, of slipping back into a version of herself that never felt good enough.

As Clara became more comfortable with The NICE Protocol, she was ready to imagine meeting her Inner Eater by walking into the room where it lived. She would begin each session by noticing her thoughts—not about food, but about weight, aging, visibility, and control. She included these thoughts in her awareness with curiosity rather than judgment, offered comfort to herself, and fully experienced the sensations in her body.

Initially, the exercise was overwhelming, and she could only stay with it for a few minutes. Her Inner Eater was raging mad at how much pressure she had felt to manage everything—her health, her appearance, her family, her image—and resentful that so much of her value seemed to hinge on staying small. She wanted rest and permission to be real, but she also feared what would happen if she let go. "I notice you're angry," she would say to her Inner Eater during these encounters. "I'm including your feelings as important, even the uncomfortable ones." Then she would offer comfort: "It makes sense you feel this way after carrying so much responsibility." Finally, she allowed herself to experience the full range of emotions—fear, grief, pressure, longing—without trying to fix or change them.

Clara wasn't surprised that her Inner Eater was upset, and she felt drawn to work with it more. It gave her something to attend to—a part of her that needed presence—not punishment. As the days passed, she began to see and speak to her Inner Eater as an orphaned part of herself, offering reassurance and warmth through each step of The NICE Protocol. She soon realized it craved connection, care, and her attention—exactly what the protocol was teaching her to provide.

After a few weeks, she invited this part of herself to leave the symbolic room and join her in her day-to-day life. She still had thoughts about her body, about regaining weight, about slipping—but they no longer controlled her. Once her Inner Eater came to live with her, she continued using The NICE Protocol not to avoid discomfort, but to be present with all the inner dialogue that had once seemed so overwhelming.

Clara was able to reduce her anxiety not by controlling her body, but by offering deep care to the part of her that had been suffering under the weight of so many untrue beliefs: that her worth was conditional, that progress was fragile, and that gaining weight meant failure. The NICE Protocol became her framework for transformation. She would notice anxiety as it arose, include it rather than fight it, comfort herself with genuine warmth, and experience the emotions without judgment.

Through this practice, anxiety became a calling card for a place inside of her that needed love and care—not a warning sign that something was wrong. Body fear wasn't a character flaw. It was a road map showing her where she could begin to offer herself understanding.

* * *

It's clear that thinking and food go together like peanut butter and jelly. But we can practice self-compassion to use toward our thinking, because it doesn't aim to directly change or eliminate thoughts. Instead, it focuses on cultivating a nonjudgmental and accepting attitude toward our thoughts, experiences, and feelings. Thoughts are natural occurrences in the mind, and struggling against them can often amplify their intensity and cause us to conclude there is an issue.

When we practice self-compassion, we acknowledge thoughts without getting caught up in them or identifying with them, which is key because we often define ourselves by our thinking. With practice, we can recognize that thoughts are not facts and that they don't define us; they are merely information. This creates a space between ourselves and our thoughts, allowing us to observe them with curiosity rather than judgment and criticism.

Self-compassion says, "You're okay even if you think your thoughts around food aren't healthy." This can help reduce the emotional charge of our thoughts, reduce the amount of food noise we experience, and lessen the impact of our thoughts on how we interact with food and how we see nourishment as a whole. For those on a GLP-1 medication, self-compassion is a reliable tool for managing the difficult emotions that come along with overthinking around food, which include our emotional math of eating. It's a superpower everyone can cultivate and has been shown by science to heal emotional pain that for so many of us is the root of emotional math. It can dissolve the harsh judgments that drive thinking and fuel mental spirals and truly create a new perspective rooted in emotional resilience. How much you think about food/eating/your body is not the issue—the judgments you have about your thinking is. And by cultivating compassionate awareness, you can develop a truly supportive relationship with yourself and how you think about food.

Chapter Takeaways
- Our culture places a high value on getting our thinking "right."
- Overthinking about food is seen as a weakness in our world.
- Adding compassion and mindfulness together is an effective tool for the judgment we have about thinking around food.
- Humans try to change the amount of thinking and the quality of their thoughts, which can be done, but it's hard and requires immense mental strength.
- The emotional math of eating is the internal weighing, measurement, evaluation, and analysis of food that everyone does.
- Most people focus on getting the correct emotional math to indicate a healthy relationship with food.
- Calling forward a clear memory or experience you have of loving something or someone else is the most effective way to get into your compassionate heart space to do compassion-focused exercises and meditations.
- When it comes to healing a relationship with food, we tend to focus on fixing a problem instead of supporting the part of us that is struggling. It takes effort and practice to change how we approach healing.
- Learning how to lovingly observe thoughts with the NICE protocol is an effective way to reduce how harshly we judge our thoughts about food.

Chapter 7

An Introduction to Reparenting

When we meet in the heart of the creator, our wounds become a
warrior's footprint, our trials and tribulations become a healing
balm, our dark night, a passage into day.
—Dr. Robert Waterman

So far, I've laid out some big ideas: how eating helps us cope with difficult experiences; how we form beliefs, often untrue, that dictate our current lives; the benefit and impact of Life Jackets; the power of self-compassion; how to meet and listen to your Inner Eater; and the emotional math we engage in around food. You may be asking yourself how these things are connected with a challenging relationship with food and your body, but they are. What happened to you, and what you believe as a result, is the beginning and end point of how you relate to food as a tool of some kind. This inner exploration will help address longstanding emotional patterns that are present but silent while you're on a GLP-1 journey to ensure lasting transformation, not just physical change.

With this foundation set, I'll introduce the concept of "reparenting" and how it can serve as a critical component of your self-care practice. With reparenting, you can give yourself what you did not receive in childhood, even though that may be hard to believe. Our hearts are hardwired for care and compassion, so even if no one taught us these things, there's a blueprint inside of us that we can call upon. The kicker is that until we believe this truth, food is an often-reached-for compensation tool. For *many* of us, food is a tool of control for feeling safe and balancing our nervous system. When life feels unsafe or out of control, we can count on food to step in and do the job. And it does. But our hearts do a better job of keeping us safe than food (or anything else we may reach for), and once we learn how, our tool kit expands. In this chapter, we'll take a deeper look at practical steps for giving ourselves the safety we may not have had growing up and why it helps our nervous system of today, and you'll learn simple techniques you can do on your own to start your reparenting journey, which will have a lifechanging impact.

What Is Reparenting?

Reparenting, also known as "healing the inner child," is a therapeutic process where you work to fulfill the emotional or physical needs that were not adequately met during your childhood. It involves recognizing that you can fulfill your own unmet needs by developing and cultivating care and connection to provide the love, safety, and guidance that may have been lacking in the past. It's like holding your own hand while you go through something scary or giving yourself emotional safety when something hard happens. Reparenting is built on the idea that our hurts are healed when we reconnect with our inner loving self, which is dependable, safe, sturdy, strong, and always available to us. You can connect to your inner child through creative intention and imagination in various ways, including writing, art, music, dance, hypnotherapy, and visualization. In this chapter we'll focus on guided meditation exercises that use imagination and visualization.

Reparenting is also a component of "parts work," a therapeutic lens that assumes we each have inner parts. Through reparenting, we can build skills to step into the role to provide safety, emotional resilience, and nurturing for ourselves, instead of depending on others or revisiting painful past experiences. It's about creating a new, safe, dependable, and loving presence within us by reconnecting our hurting inner parts with our compassionate heart, also known as our loving self or soul self.

Including reparenting in a self-compassion model is particularly effective for healing emotional eating, because it addresses the root issue of unmet emotional needs often met by food. Reparenting helps us emotionally regulate old parts of ourselves that drive our primary relationship with food, creating a regulated, balanced nervous system in the present day.

There are two approaches to reparenting: self-directed or with a licensed therapist. We'll be utilizing self-directed reparenting, which you can do through various exercises and visualizations. Now you may wonder how this could possibly be related to your relationship with food and dismiss it as just another self-help trend. However, self-care through reparenting is some of the most challenging work you can do. Being in touch with hurting parts of yourself is uncomfortable, and it might even be scary. But deciding you are worth the effort of deep self-care is necessary, useful, and healing. Often, willpower around eating is emphasized as the key to change, when in reality, the key is just the opposite: trusting that *you* can provide the safety and comfort you seek from food.

My Reparenting Story

In the summer of 1992, while still in college, I engaged in a period of self-reflection. One day, I stumbled upon a PBS show featuring John Bradshaw discussing his book *Homecoming: Reclaiming and Championing Your Inner Child*. He spoke of our "wounded inner child," which resulted from growing up in dysfunctional families, a concept that resonated deeply with me and sparked an outpouring of suppressed emotions.

At nineteen, I became acutely aware of a profound well of pain within me, a seeming abyss that I feared I might fall into and never return from. However, Bradshaw's words helped me comprehend my pain's source and why I felt compelled to distance myself from it. I had always believed that moving away from my childhood pain was the path to healing, but Bradshaw was the first to encourage me to find the strength to even consider the idea that healing could be found by moving closer to my emotional pain. What I didn't know then was how my habits around food (eating, not eating, bingeing, dieting) were all effective tools to distance me from the near-constant emotional pain I felt from childhood. Bradshaw's PBS special was one of the first frameworks I found that felt doable for confronting the pain that, at the time, I had no idea how to manage.

Eager to explore this further, I bought Bradshaw's book, along with Louise Hay's *You Can Heal Your Life*. That summer, I first encountered the scared, lonely, and abandoned child within me. Honestly, she took up so much space that I thought she was *all* of me, not just a part of me. Until that point, I had concentrated on not drowning in pain—keeping it at arm's length to have breathable space just to live a bit normally. My focus was on distancing my internal pain and shunning vulnerability. Joy? Peace? Thriving? Those were for everyone else. I was focused on making sure the walls did not cave in, and the thought of the sunshine streaming in through a window of my inner room was a dream I held in secret—too big of an ask for my life as it was. And until my dream might manifest by a miracle bestowed upon me, food was my tool for soothing myself.

In those early adult years, I became an expert at "adopting" the mothers of my closest friends. I would hang on to every word my friends shared about their mothers, watch how they interacted with their families, and try to be included in all their genuinely happy households. All the while, I was carrying my dark secret: I was a throwaway child, and if you got to know me—really got to know me—you too would discover it's probably best to throw me away. But through those early glimpses into Bradshaw's and Hay's books, the seed was planted: I could identify my childhood pain and potentially heal it through reparenting. I continued searching for substitute mothers in friendships, mentors, bosses, and relationships. This process stretched over nearly three decades. Eventually, I was introduced to my teacher, Dr. Robert Waterman. Over the last twenty years of working with him as a student and intern, he showed me how to love myself and helped me believe I could face my pain. But initially it took some years before I was finally able to put this technique into practice. Terrified of unlocking unmanageable pain and having it take over my life, I saw loving my hurting parts as a last resort. Why dig up the past? Why focus on things I couldn't change? However, it got to the point that no other healing tools were working for me.

I felt stuck and yearned to be free from the constant dread and anxiety that had become my companions. Emotional intimacy triggered overwhelming panic and debilitating dread, while vulnerability in relationships and friendships set off uncontrollable fight-or-flight responses. To dull the dread, I created a constellation of coping mechanisms: binge eating, shopping, seeking social status, hobbies, perfectionism, and even spirituality. None of them provided lasting relief, and the persistent anxiety prevented me from having the fulfilling relationships I desired, so I decided to go inward and make peace with the dread. Since I had exhausted all options to numb or hide it, I committed to working with the discomfort until it subsided. The first time I tried this process, I was only aware of the feeling of dread itself, not its origin or the part of me that needed reparenting. (I often see this with my clients as well: They feel emotional discomfort but can't identify a specific age or event to work with.) I simply leaned into the dread with compassion, trusting it would lead me to the part that needed care. This trust proved to be highly effective. While it may seem obvious to lean into the dread, our hurt parts often create narratives about why they need to remain untouched. Feeling damaged by my dread, anxiety, and childhood, I had convinced myself I was beyond help, even from my own heart.

I created a schedule to work with the dread—after dinner, alone in the bathtub. Initially, this felt awkward and strange, but I persisted. I would sit in the warm water, visualizing my heart connecting with the dread. After a few days with minimal results, my birth date suddenly popped into my head. I'm an identical twin, and my sister and I were born two months premature. While I knew I had birth trauma, when I was growing up, everyone focused on our lucky survival, so I didn't realize its deep connection to my attachment and intimacy issues. Back then, ultrasounds didn't exist, and our heartbeats were synchronized, so no one knew my mom was carrying twins! As soon as we were born, we were separated into incubators and transferred to a hospital over an hour away from our parents. For more than a month, I wasn't nursed, was held only sporadically, and was separated from my twin. This is where I would begin: caring for myself as a preemie baby.

Over a number of weeks, I stepped into the bathtub, engaged my compassionate heart and loving self, and visited my preemie self. I imagined holding, feeding, singing, rocking, clothing, and loving my little self. Intense emotions arose: sadness, anger, grief, rage, confusion. I imagined holding myself as a baby, telling her how much I loved her, how much she meant to me, that she hadn't done anything wrong, and that she would be okay. I loved and held her for weeks. As my baby-self felt loved, the dread lifted. That was eight years ago—and the dread is still gone.

I then decided to confront a much more traumatic moment from my childhood: when I said goodbye to my mother at six years old after my parents divorced. It felt like the most significant day of my existence, bringing me the closest I had ever been to the feeling of death. My sister and I were leaving our mother behind and would never live with her again. A big black car took us to the airport, and all the while, I wished for the journey to stretch out indefinitely, so we wouldn't have to say goodbye. Anxiety, dread, fear, and profound sadness overwhelmed me. I was consumed by the few remaining minutes I had with my mother.

Upon reaching the airport, the finality of the impending goodbye hit us hard. My sister, unable to contain her distress, started vomiting at the airport gate. Our sobbing seemed to catch our mother off guard, and she quickly ran out of tissues. All I could think was, *Why is this happening? Why is my life with her being taken away? How could my mother agree to this? What did I do to deserve such a fate? How can I possibly bear this pain?* Confused and traumatized, my sister and I boarded the plane... alone and motherless.

I imagined what would be useful, helpful, and supportive to give my little self on the day she said goodbye to her mother. I spent months with my hurting parts, even creating a schedule to be with them. It wasn't complicated; I just revisited the painful memory, supplementing it with love, support, and compassion for my younger self going through that painful event. This imaginative process involved comforting my younger self, holding her hand, soothing her, singing to her, and reassuring her of my presence as she faced a daunting challenge. I would listen to her fears, visualize her as the frightened child she was, and hold her in my arms, offering solace. Often, we cried together. But I assured her that she hadn't done anything wrong and that I'd always be there for her; most important, I created a felt sense of security and attachment between us, which helped regulate both our nervous systems.

The initial stages of this self-reparenting process were intense, emotionally taxing, and filled with sadness. But over time, with constant revisiting and comforting, the profound grief has been replaced by a manageable amount of sadness that doesn't disrupt my nervous system like it used to. I no longer compensate for it like I used to. It feels neutral now. Although the memory of saying goodbye to my mother still stings a bit, it no longer overwhelms me.

I've repeated this reparenting process hundreds of times across various experiences, and they all shared some similarities. Initially, I craved assurance of a specific outcome. I tried to make it transactional, thinking, "If I spend an hour tonight reparenting myself, I want 10 percent less anxiety tomorrow." I earnestly bargained with the Universe, fearing a lack of control, like jumping out of a plane without knowing if the parachute would open. I wanted the guarantee of a safe return from visiting my hurting parts before I'd even begin. Of course, I did! That's human nature—to seek reassurance.

Now, however, I understand that this resistance is part of the process, and I'm accustomed to my ego's pushback. My advice is to start small, pace yourself, and most important, seek help from an experienced clinician if you feel overwhelmed.

The Evolution of Reparenting and Inner Child Work

Many years after reading Bradshaw's book on reparenting, I discovered its roots in Carl Jung's work. Jung, a pioneering psychologist, introduced the idea of the "inner child," a part of our subconscious that holds our earliest experiences and learnings and is shaped by innate "primordial images" present from birth. These images, part of our collective unconscious, deeply influence our behaviors and interactions, especially if they carry trauma or anxiety from those early years.

Jung believed we have unconscious thoughts and desires—separate parts of ourselves with their own beliefs and motivations—that can influence our behaviors, particularly around eating, without us realizing it. For instance, a part of us associated with comfort or security might lead to emotional eating during stressful times, even if we consciously desire to eat healthier. Similarly, a part of us focused on self-worth or body image might drive restrictive eating patterns despite our conscious intentions. By understanding these unconscious motivations, we gain insight into our eating behaviors and can develop strategies to address them more effectively.

Jungian psychotherapy aims to heal this inner child through reparenting, helping individuals work through their inner child's trauma. Reparenting, which you can do yourself, as I did, helps you break free from negative subconscious patterns, leading to a healthier life, a regulated nervous system, and better emotional resilience.

Jung's work also laid the groundwork for other approaches, like Internal Family Systems (IFS), shadow work, and inner child work. These approaches share similarities and overlap, but I emphasize compassion as the central guiding principle for healing here. Reparenting with self-compassion at its core is remembering our innate wholeness, even when life events make us feel broken. Troubles with food and a negative body image can hinder this remembrance and remind us of a part of ourselves needing attention. Our loving presence, caring for our hurting parts, is a powerful reminder that nothing, not even our birth, is beyond our care, love, and compassion.

It's Never Too Late to Give Yourself Safety

I want to invite you to consider a young person who must take care of themselves after school. At thirteen years old, they walk home from school, let themselves into the house, make a snack, and keep themselves busy until their parents get home at dinnertime. If something happens while they're at home by themselves, they're left on their own to handle the situation. So, if they're making a pizza snack and cheese melts onto the bottom of the toaster oven, causing it to start smoking and setting off the smoke alarm, they only have their thirteen-year-old brain to decide how best to handle that. If they had a bad day at school and got into an argument with their friend, they may want to sit in front of the television and eat a bag of potato chips and decide not to stop until the bag is empty. It would be logical to say that a thirteen-year-old should not be expected to know how to handle complex issues that arise the same way an adult does.

I'm using a simple analogy here because it's easy to imagine the difference if an adult were present, helping the child navigate the situation, saying encouraging things, soothing their fears about the smoke alarm, putting the potato chips in a small bowl rather than handing them the whole bag. Can a thirteen-year-old be at home alone? Sure. If things go wrong when that child is alone, will they handle it in the best way they can? Sure. Will their actions be ideal? Maybe not.

That is a great analogy for looking at your life: How many times were you challenged by some kind of event and did the best you could but still suffered as a result? How many experiences did you have where you would have benefited from a kind, mature, loving adult? It may be easy to blame our caregivers at first and assume that if they had just done things differently—been more involved, evolved, or prepared—our lives would be different.

As you're learning in this book, you can't change the past, but you *can* add in the care you didn't receive (even if it was long ago), and it will create a felt sense of safety in your body now instead of using food to do it. What if the thirteen-year-old in this story was you? Could you imagine how different that kid's nervous system would be if they came home from school and adult-you were there? When the smoke alarm went off, for instance, you would tell them everything was under control, and they didn't need to worry or feel bad.

You can practice this by looking back on events in your own life like chapters in a book and see how your younger self may have felt alone, afraid, or abandoned, and how that self could now benefit from your support. Instead of hoping caregivers or partners will suddenly come to your rescue, you can do it yourself.

Why Reparenting Is a Valuable Process

I've explained how we use food to cope with overwhelming or uncomfortable emotions, often driven by untrue beliefs about ourselves (yet we build entire self-care systems around them!). And how extending kindness and forgiveness toward ourselves and the misunderstandings causing emotional dysregulation can improve our relationship with food and our body. Reparenting is a wonderful way to take these skills and go deeper.

Taking what you've learned so far, we're going to time-travel and expand your healing path. With reparenting, you can move your loving awareness to any past event or memory and lay a new foundation of safety, care, comfort, and connection. This regulates the nervous system then and now, but more important, it reminds the old, isolated parts that were in charge of your safety when you were younger that they're not alone, they never were, and you are now here to help them.

This inner resourcing helps clear up the misunderstandings that your relationship with food is managing and helps your parts experience being connected to something bigger than the limited viewpoint they are operating under. Reparenting is peeling back layers of life; compassionately peering into hard events where you may have felt afraid, alone, or abandoned; and loving those parts of you. It's an active process.

Reparenting is reconnecting parts of you with your loving self, which is the inner place where safety lives—but it's also the place we get disconnected from during hard life events. When you take the time to lovingly ask the parts inside of you what happened to them and what they need, and then tell them how sorry you are it's been a challenge and that they're not alone, they heal.

From this larger viewpoint of care, our issues around eating, food and our body image may have seemed like burdens needing solving. But they are actually helpers that can guide us to love parts inside us that feel isolated and alone and are running on stories full of self-judgment and self-persecution.

Starting your reparenting journey around food and your body might sound something like this: "I've had a history of eating to cope with overwhelming feelings. I'm going to take a minute to explore more about the part of me that has felt overwhelmed and why. What does it need from me? How long has it felt like that? What happened to it?"

One of my favorite metaphors for reparenting and emotional eating is teaching a child to ride a bike, which has all the components of living life, such as challenges, wisdom building, and nervous system regulation. Learning to ride involves multiple components: balance, pedaling, steering, navigating bumps, and avoiding collisions. They all need to happen simultaneously, requiring practice and self-confidence. For a young person, aligning all these skills can be a challenge, especially at first. When teaching a child to ride, we know falls are common, and these can be frustrating and scary. Scary experiences dysregulate a child's nervous system, triggering a need for reassurance. Imagine a crying, scared child running to you after falling. They want to give up, have you do it for them, or end the uncomfortable process altogether. What would you do? The kind and loving response would be to comfort them, holding them until they calm down. You're not scared or upset; you have full confidence they'll learn. You provide a safe space for their distress, allowing their nervous system to regulate. Once calm, they wipe away their tears, look up, and declare they're ready to try again.

Think for a moment what would happen if that child didn't receive words of encouragement, comfort, care, or love. They might turn on themselves and say unkind things, their nervous system might go into fight-or-flight mode, or they might give up on bike riding altogether.

The child doesn't have the maturity or brain development yet to know how to handle or navigate hard events, so they look to their caregivers to guide, nurture, and love them. This regulates their nervous systems and, more important, means they won't then internalize negative thoughts about themselves. This mirrors how we reparent ourselves. We offer our inner parts a safe space to re-regulate their nervous systems, fostering safety and connection, so they can continue on their path. We create an environment of connection and love, allowing their nervous systems to recover. We don't "do" much, but we maintain a state of being safe, loving, calm, warm, and confident. Maybe we offer hugs, reassurance, gentle rocking, or care for their physical scrapes. Most of all, we provide a safe refuge while they learn a challenging skill.

Deep care, love, and connection regulate a child's nervous system, enabling them to get back on the bike. Similarly, reparenting our inner parts allows us to face challenges with greater resilience and self-compassion. This may seem counterintuitive, because if life has been hard, going inward can seem like the last place to find emotional safety and resilience, yet it is.

The Power of Your Loving Presence

What events in your life do you think would benefit from self-care? Most of us have faced big challenges and felt alone or afraid. We can't change events that have already happened, but those experiences largely inform how we live our lives right now. Reparenting is a great tool that uses imagination and visualization to connect with and support parts of ourselves from different times in our lives when we felt challenged and alone.

Have you ever had a friend hold your hand before surgery or an important job interview? They likely told you everything was going to be fine, that you weren't alone. Reparenting is just like that, except you visualize connecting with a younger part of yourself instead of a friend. To do this, first ask yourself, "How would I care for a hurting friend?" Then, to move into your reparenting self, ask, "How would I care for my hurting part?" or "What does my hurting part need that I can give it?"

I've found that our parts that hold big emotions like hurt, fear, or anger mostly want to be seen and heard. They want connection. They want to know they're not alone. They want to be loved. Your loving presence is the healing that your parts want and need to regulate their nervous systems. This is key for healing your relationship with food and your body, because it's a way to compensate for the pain or discomfort you try to solve with eating. Instead of using food, relationships, money, or a job, you can take care of your needs and emotionally regulate your parts in a deeply compassionate way. All you need is willingness, imagination, and stepping into your compassionate heart.

Because reparenting is a therapeutic process that allows us to reexperience childhood feelings and develop a nurturing parental voice within ourselves, it's an effective framework for healing emotional pain. One of the biggest benefits is that it regulates the nervous systems of our younger parts, which are often dysregulated from traumatic experiences. This translates into a more regulated nervous system in the present. Self-compassion is vital in this process, as it helps us acknowledge our pain, validate our emotions, and provide ourselves with the understanding and care we may have lacked in childhood. Children have a limited capacity to understand trauma, so they often turn a challenging event into something they are responsible for. Developmentally, this is expected because the prefrontal cortex has not yet developed. But energetically, we stay at that age, paralyzed by the overwhelm we may have felt back then. More than two-thirds of all children in the United States have experienced at least one traumatic event by sixteen; some events are bigger than others. But no matter your experience, how hard things were, or what you decided, you can change your mind and start living the life you want.

By engaging the disconnected, younger, neglected parts of you with deep care and compassion, the parts of yourself that hold misconceptions about your innate goodness can heal. This profoundly changes how you relate to food for safety and comfort. When, with deep compassion, you engage the disconnected, younger, cast-out parts of yourself that believe untrue things about your innate goodness, those parts can be coaxed into the present, positively impacting your relationship with food and your body, offering a more lasting healing for post-GLP1 life.

Exercise: Give Yourself What You Didn't Receive

One of the largest challenges of taking the plunge to give yourself emotional safety is recognizing that it's not done through intellect, mind, or willpower: It's done through the experience of your heart. In this exercise, you'll think of a time when you felt that your emotional needs were not met by others, and you'll practice fulfilling them yourself. This is an imaginative, heartfelt process in which you will imagine cultivating and extending caring feelings toward yourself at an earlier age.

It's worth noting that some sadness or grief may be involved as you give yourself what you didn't receive in the past. It may be sad to visit parts of yourselves that have been neglected or hurt. You may feel big emotions. If your emotions start to feel too big as you work on this exercise, you know it's time to pull in the help of a professional.

When I do this work, I always set aside at least thirty minutes when I won't be disturbed. I center myself, taking deep breaths to move into my compassionate heart, and then I imagine walking into the scene where I find my little self. It's powerful, emotional, and freeing. I still cry almost every time I work with hurting parts of myself. But the pain of living with hurting parts trying to manage things they simply can't has blocked me from the goals I want to reach. I do reparenting exercises with different parts of myself until I don't feel intense emotions anymore, which sometimes takes hours, weeks, or months.

I believe you can do this. When you do, it will heal your life and relationships. You are the one you are looking for, and all the issues with food and your body are helping you to remember that.

Let's begin:

- Think about a time in your life when you felt alone, and your nervous system felt dysregulated because of how alone you felt. Ease your way into this, and don't use the most painful events in your life to practice this. Sit in a place where you won't be disturbed, review the following instructions, and then close your eyes to let your imagination guide you. (It's helpful to read this exercise a few times before you practice it.)
- Once you've remembered a time when you felt alone, ask yourself the following: "Do I believe I can give myself the care I never received?" and "If not, will I try to cultivate and give myself care in this exercise?"
- Next, take a few deep, relaxing breaths.
- Place your focus and awareness on your physical heart, and then imagine focusing on your compassionate heart, which is the place inside of you where love and compassion are created and flow out. Because your heart beats, this place exists.

- Imagine being surrounded by care and love in your compassionate heart. What does it feel like? Take a moment to pause here and let that feeling soak into every cell of your body, surrounding you like a warm blanket.

- See yourself walking out of your compassionate heart space, still infused with the feeling of care and love, and imagine walking into a large field of beautiful flowers. The sun is warm and bright, and the sky is clear and blue. On the other side of the field of flowers, see the version of you that feels alone or has experienced not having their needs met. Start walking toward them.

- As you approach yourself, imagine with all your heart that you have exactly what they need to feel less alone. Inside of you is the magic key to feeling connected, cared for, and less alone.

- Tell the younger you: "I am here to care for you, and you will not be alone anymore." Notice what the younger you experiences and feels as you say that.

- Notice that your very presence heals the aloneness. You know exactly how your younger self feels; you lived it too. Tap into the care and compassion you feel in every cell of your body and gently hold their hand. What do you notice? What do you feel?

- Imagine now spending some time in the field of flowers with the younger you, being present, caring, and loving. Your presence and understanding provide safety and heal the aloneness.

- Let the younger you know they haven't done anything wrong, and you will never leave them. Consider compassionate words of encouragement, such as "You haven't done anything wrong" or "I am so sorry you had to experience this." And then ask, "What do you need right now?

- Next, check in with your present-day, adult nervous system. How is it doing? As you bring awareness to both your younger and current selves, tap into your compassionate heart again. Notice that the care flows and flows and won't run out.

- Thank the younger you for visiting and let them know you will come back to see them again. Alternatively, you can bring them back home with you to live with you now. Either option works. See yourself walking back through the field of flowers (with them if they decide to come). Walk back into your compassionate heart space, then your physical heart, and then your breath. After a few deep breaths, open your eyes and take your time getting up.

You are practicing being present with parts of yourself that did not receive emotional safety and providing that safety, and that is the secret sauce for healing emotional eating. You are giving safety to yourself instead of using food to do it. As I've mentioned a few times, this helps regulate the nervous systems of the younger parts of you as well as your present self. Emotional eating is rooted in a lack of emotional safety and often pulls you out of the present—where you can make healthy decisions for yourself.

So often, your younger parts that did not receive safety and security get locked in time—frozen, if you will—with whatever belief they created to stay safe. But your care is enough to unfreeze and free them. This exercise allows you to have a direct experience and dialogue with parts of you, so that they feel safe again, and let go of protective beliefs that drive your emotional eating.

Martin's Story

Martin came to see me for his stress eating. He had multiple health issues that were worsening over time, and he was using food to soothe and reward himself and wanted to stop. His stress eating was keeping extra weight on his body that he didn't want, destabilizing his blood sugar levels, and keeping him in a shame cycle about his choices and perceived lack of willpower, because he knew how and what he was "supposed" to be eating.

The few times Martin had lost weight, he had grappled with feeling like an impostor and eventually gained the weight back. He worked long hours at his emotionally demanding finance job. Exhausted at the end of each day, he often felt immense pressure to juggle life, and it felt overwhelming to always make nutritious food choices. This created tremendous guilt, which he knew wasn't helpful. When he was thinner, he felt like an impostor. When he was bigger, he felt stuck in shame about his perceived lack of willpower. He couldn't stop judging himself for lacking motivation to make fresh, healthy food and prioritize his health. On top of this, he had experienced a lifetime of a chronic illness that caused a lot of pain.

Martin was also on a GLP-1 medication, which had helped reduce his cravings and obsessive thoughts about food. But it didn't fix the emotional root of his eating patterns, and he feared what would happen if it stopped working.

This is a wonderful example of how often highly intelligent men and women, who have an accurate grasp of their goals and clear reasoning about why they aren't reaching them, don't understand the specific steps to change. In Martin's case, he thought it was a lack of willpower and responsibility and wanted me to help him find the secret formula that would solve his problems.

Like most clients I work with, Martin assumed he was to blame or was missing something like a fancy new skill or mindset strategy to meet his challenge and make new "healthy" habits. He was looking to reduce thoughts and actions around stress eating as a sign of healing and success, and he'd try to will his brain into letting go of the thoughts that were holding him back from his goals. He really thought that one day, when he got the formula "right" or his body to a certain size, his relationship with life would be transformed.

Martin felt a certain amount of urgency for change, because his health issues were becoming more complicated and debilitating, and he was convinced that if he couldn't "eat in a way that supports my health," his health would worsen, and it would be his fault if that happened. By the time we met, he felt fully responsible for his worsening health condition and increased stress eating—and was convinced his lack of intelligence was to blame. He believed that his chronic illness was his fault, and that if he wasn't "perfect," he was failing. Because of this, he blamed himself for being weak and causing everything to go "wrong."

Because of how ingrained it was, Martin didn't see how his self-blame left no room for cooperation with his health challenges, where he could make big changes in his relationship with food. Martin had created his entire relationship with food and himself based on bad data, believing something was wrong with him and that he was weak. He thought his eating was something to solve, cure, and resolve as a measurement of personal success. He had jumped from protocol to protocol, looking for the best way to take care of his eating, chronic illness, and stress. And now that fear included the worry his GLP-1 medication would stop working or stall.

Martin's approach to reversing his relationship with food and his body was built upon his core belief that he was weak and that being perfect would keep him safe. Consciously, he thought he was moving past it by trying to create a solution to his problem (which is what cognitive behavioral therapy does). However, he couldn't yet see that the way he was "solving" his problem still included the root of the problem: that he was the cause and that something was wrong with him. But I believed there could be more to his drive to find the "perfect" relationship with food for emotional safety, and I also wondered if using self-compassion and reparenting could help widen his perspective and lift his self-persecution approach.

When I gently asked Martin what would happen if he wasn't to blame for his health problems, he seemed confused. He hadn't considered that possibility because blaming himself helped him make sense of the pain he was experiencing and made it logical. He reasoned, "I got a horrible disease; I must have done something wrong." Getting sick without a cause would be so vague it would cause more emotional dysregulation than believing he was at fault. Not blaming himself would touch on his spiritual beliefs and sense of order in the world. He might think, "Would God punish me by giving me this disease for no reason? That would make me so mad, but I can't be mad at God. God only punishes people who deserve it. So I must be to blame. Maybe if I'm perfect, God won't punish me anymore." He had solidified the distorted life view created to make sense of a difficult hand that life had dealt him through the chronic illness, and all solutions to ease the pain around this life view flowed through his core beliefs that "it's my fault" and "I must be perfect to stay safe."

Martin and I began to explore the impact of self-blame and perfectionism on his health. When asked what might happen if he didn't blame himself or strive for perfection, Martin insisted that he must take charge of his health by eating perfectly, as any deviation led to health issues and weight gain. This belief was reinforced by his doctors with the message he heard in appointments that "good patients who care about their health make healthy choices to support their health." Martin asserted that everyone is responsible for their own health, and poor health is a result of personal failure.

To challenge this perspective, I pointed out the difference between being in charge of one's health and blaming oneself for bad health. When he struggled to see this distinction, I explained that his decisions about eating were based on a flawed belief that he was to blame for his health problems. This belief, formed during childhood, acted like a "programming virus" in his "life computer system." He had internalized the idea that being perfect kept him safe, especially in the emotionally turbulent environment of his childhood.

Martin's childhood had been marked by emotional rigidity, yelling, and a lack of safety. His father, a former military officer, believed that order and perfection were the only protections against chaos. Mistakes weren't just corrected—they were punished. Martin blamed himself for these issues, believing that being a perfect son could have prevented them. Although he now logically understood that it wasn't his fault, the emotional impact persisted. Over time, this emotional template became second nature—so familiar and automatic that it felt like common sense. This session introduced the idea that blaming himself for his chronic illness might be an extension of his childhood coping mechanisms.

When asked if he felt something hard and hostile was happening now, Martin admitted that his chronic health issues felt like a personal failure. He had been punishing himself and striving for a perfect lifestyle to make things right. I explained that such coping mechanisms, built on self-blame, would eventually break down, leading to emotional distress. From a self-compassion and reparenting perspective, it was essential for him to recognize that his emotional pain stemmed from incorrect beliefs about himself.

I explained that his programming virus had distorted his view of life, food, and illness. I emphasized that letting go of self-blame and striving for perfection might seem counterintuitive, because these behaviors had become ingrained as safety mechanisms. However, true healing would come from understanding that he was not to blame and had done nothing wrong.

Martin resonated with the idea that his "issues" could be indicators of a need for self-compassion rather than flaws. He realized that his eating patterns might be an alarm clock, reminding him to care for himself. This shift in perspective made him feel less overwhelmed by his eating habits.

I suggested the reparenting exercise that follows to help nurture the younger version of himself who felt responsible for everything. Martin agreed to try this, recognizing the potential for positive change in his self-perception and relationship with food, but like most of us, the idea of facing any kind of pain was daunting and seemed counterintuitive. *It wasn't indulgent. It was necessary.* I want to emphasize this for a moment: Humans do not want to feel pain, ever. Especially emotional pain. Our brain sends strong signals when we feel emotional pain to help make it stop. Like a neon sign blinking "DANGER!" But, to untie the emotional knot of pain holding us back from the life we desire, we have to face it, and this was the case for Martin. Up until now, he didn't know how. We spent a bit of time discussing this, because the thought of facing pain and comforting himself seemed not only indulgent but also scary. As you read this, know that this is part of the process and consider the old phrase "the best way forward is through." Remember, most of us fear pain of any kind, and our minds actively shield us from moving toward pain. That is the reason the heart (not the mind) works so well for reparenting. This shift toward being *with* emotional pain instead of fixing it is not an intellectual task. It's a bodily experience. A felt experience. A process of the heart. Like the warmth you feel when someone tells you they love you. It takes practice, patience, and an honest recognition that, for many of us, it goes against everything we've learned. It can even feel unsafe. But it's how we begin to feel at home with ourselves.

I walked Martin through a process much like the birth story I shared earlier in the chapter. He wanted to change his "computer programming virus" and dedicated time each day to nurture the younger version of himself by using his heart, not his mind. After years of wanting change and trying to change through willpower without results, Martin was motivated to try something different. Together, we created a schedule to nurture the younger version of himself who felt responsible for everything. When he leaned in and imagined what this younger version might look and feel like, a 14-year-old version of himself appeared in his mind's eye. He looked tired, anxious, and scared. When Martin felt his presence, he switched into "compassion mode" by feeling what it would be like to be with him throughout the day, such as while driving to and from work or eating dinner at night. The switch from mind to heart was not to ask or change anything in himself or his younger part—he would simply extend the feelings of kindness, caring, and curiosity to this younger part of himself and hang out without feeling like he needed to change anything.

Like we had discussed, the most challenging part of this process was feeling the discomfort from emotional pain that surfaced when visiting with his younger part and trusting the process. But we had normalized this through our sessions together and Martin expected this to come forward, so he wasn't surprised—only uncomfortable. The goal was to welcome his younger self to be with him in a safe, warm, and inviting space through connection and compassion. I told him to imagine as best he could that his younger part was like an orphan who had no home and just needed his company and to feel safe and that would be enough. Martin had to consciously dedicate time and energy each day to this process and release expectations about how this would turn out, such as getting better health and eating habits as a result. In just a few weeks of practicing reparenting this part of himself, he noticed less self-blame and reported a general sense of calm, connection, and neutrality. He still felt self-perfection on occasion but now had a practiced set of skills to not judge self-perfection when it surfaced. "Oh, self-perfection, you're back. This is hard and feels horrible. There must be a layer coming up for me around this that needs soothing and comforting." This was massive progress for Martin, because prior to his learning these skills, his first thought was always, "You are a piece of shit. Try harder, stupid. This is all your fault." He was learning how to move toward the discomfort inside himself and building trust that he was fully able and capable of managing it, and the harsh words of the past came from judging himself as a way to handle the pain. *He didn't need to earn rest anymore.* Now he had a better way of handling pain, and as a result, he was gentler with himself when he struggled. Life seemed less against him from this new perspective, and he had a solid set of skills to apply when it came up. His health struggles morphed from the narrative that life was punishing to life was asking for him to go deeper into himself for care. The fear that his GLP-1 medication may stop working stopped feeling so overwhelming, because he was learning how to sit with the discomfort without slipping into harsh self-persecution. In the past, food was a way to get a break from that punishment, but now his own comfort was a resource he could trust, and because of that, the relationship with his health, food, and body improved.

Exercise: Get Started Practicing Reparenting

- Make a list of at least five events that have happened in your life that caused you to feel dysregulated or isolated.
- For each event listed, ask yourself, "On a scale of 1 to 10 (10 being the highest), how alone did I feel?"
- Take a few deep breaths and visualize your heart. Say to yourself, "I'm going to imagine connecting with a part inside of me that is struggling or hurting, and I'm going to treat that part just like I would a friend who is struggling. I'm going to be curious about what it might need from me that I can give."
- Ask yourself if you'd be willing to nurture or care for the part you discover inside of you. If so, then ask what that younger part might need or want that you can give it. Can you imagine giving what's needed to the part of you that is struggling, hurt, sad, confused, or alone?
- How would you view your life or that event differently if you had had more loving, caring support?
- Is there anything you are afraid of that might prevent you from giving your younger part safety and security?

* * *

Old pain will find a way to attract your attention through things like anxiety, depression, and perceived failures (and of course emotional eating!) so that, eventually, you will care for it, transform it, and bring it home to your heart. But usually, before you see it like that, pain may just seem like punishment. When we encounter old pain (even briefly), alarm bells may go off in our nervous system. The process of moving *toward pain* instead of *away from it* is uncomfortable. It's helpful to know this, so you aren't surprised.

Remember, how and what we eat is often a stress response or coping mechanism for uncomfortable emotions, so it's natural to have a knee-jerk reaction to shy away from this process. More than that, you may have an inner voice saying, "Don't stir this pot; you're about to make things worse." If that statement deeply resonates with you, you can craft some self-compassionate words of reassurance like "Of course warning bells are going off and it feels like things might get worse if I compassionately reparent myself. I will be okay. I can do this."

Reparenting with self-compassion allows you to heal these past traumas and hurting inner parts, develop the confidence to provide your own emotional safety in the present and future, and transform your relationship with food. Like self-compassion, reparenting requires trust, vulnerability, and practice. If you decide to begin reparenting parts of yourself, start small and go slow. Enlist the help of an experienced reparenting or parts work practitioner, if needed. Remember, you can start the reparenting process by focusing on a specific event or by simply tuning in to a feeling that will lead you to a part of yourself that needs attention.

I define *healing* as being present with pain and reconciling it with care. Healing is remembering that our heart is the safe haven, no matter what's happened to us. We have been conditioned to think otherwise so much so that often it's hard to believe we are worth our own effort. Yet we are. We can offer ourselves what we didn't receive, and our heart is not only hardwired to do this but also waiting to. Each time we vote for ourselves and take steps to be with our hurt parts, we move away from needing food to do it for us and instead trust that our heart can. No matter how long we've used food for soothing ourselves, we can call upon our heart to step in at any time. Love is the medicine, and our heart is the pharmacy.

Chapter Takeaways

- Reparenting means taking care of yourself in a loving and caring way. It's stepping in to
- be your own safe self, providing emotional safety for times you didn't receive it, and reconnecting to your loving-soul self where safety is alive and well.
- An easy way to start reparenting with self-compassion is to ask yourself, "How would I care for a hurting friend?" Then ask, "How would I care for my hurting part?" or "What does my hurting part need that I can give it?"
- Our inner parts often have dysregulated nervous systems that are impacting the nervous system of today that we are trying to regulate with food. No matter how long ago your nervous

system became dysregulated, you can regulate it now through the power of your heart.

- The essential ingredients to reparenting are imagination, visualization, and intention.
- You might identify either a specific "part" of yourself to reparent or a feeling that you can explore that will lead you to that part. Being with your hurt parts requires intention, time, presence, and kindness.
- Love and care for yourself are not bound by space or time, so you can go back to a time when you didn't receive the care you wanted or needed and apply it by connecting with your loving heart.
- Reparenting is an inward journey through which you reconnect to your loving self to solve issues and heal.
- You can learn and practice reparenting exercises yourself, but it's normal to encounter emotional discomfort during this process; if it's too intense, seek help from a licensed therapist.
- Self-compassion, at its core, is a reparenting tool.

Chapter 8

Challenges with Food Help You Love Parts in You That Hurt

I saw that the divine beauty in each heart is the root of all
time and space.
—Rabia

Is it possible that challenges with food and your body could guide you to become more loving toward yourself? Instead of problems to be solved, what if they were messengers guiding you to a more peaceful existence? Most of us have been conditioned to view these challenges as battles to win—evidence of personal failure or weakness that we must overcome through discipline and willpower. But what if these struggles were actually invitations? Invitations to remember you have always been whole and worthy from the very beginning of your life.

Perhaps challenges with food and your body are simply unexpected guides, illuminating the places within that have forgotten your inherent value. Imagine if what you've labeled as "problems" could become allies, leading you back to the places inside that have forgotten this truth. For those on GLP-1 medications, this perspective is especially powerful. These medications act as "room movers," creating precious space between physical hunger and the emotional patterns that drive so much pain. With the breathing room these medications provide, you have an unprecedented opportunity to explore and heal your relationship with yourself in ways that were previously obscured by constant food noise and cravings. And yet, the unknowns can feel daunting. What does the future hold on this medication? What if it stops working or something goes wrong?

My own journey of reparenting my inner child transformed how I understand food and my body. Where I once only saw weakness and failure, I began to recognize unmet needs crying out for attention. At first, I thought they were crying out for my parents' attention, which was continually disappointing. But they were actually crying out for *my* attention and care. By learning and then offering myself the same compassion and understanding I would give a child learning to ride a bike—celebrating small victories, and compassionate guidance after falls—I developed a relationship with myself built on trust rather than criticism. This foundation supported changes that willpower alone never could.

In this chapter, we'll explore how to approach healing from abundance rather than lack or scarcity. We'll also examine why fear and shame—though common motivators for change—ultimately undermine lasting transformation. And, we'll practice specific reparenting tools that nurture self-trust and acceptance, creating a relationship with food that reflects your true worth rather than reinforcing old wounds.

An Opportunity for Profound Healing

We start life with a clean slate—giving and receiving love in an even exchange. But then something happens, like having an emotionally abusive parent, and the love we offer isn't reciprocated. So, to compensate, we give even more love, hoping to receive love back. But we don't. In fact, the abusive parent might tell us they wish we had never been born or that all their bad luck is because of us or that we'll never amount to anything. The clean slate of giving and receiving love is shattered and replaced by a hostile battlefield.

In an effort to regulate and find normalcy during battle, we learn the battlefield system: We do things like abandon ourselves to caretake our parents or manipulate others to gain power and stability. We look for safety outside of ourselves because we innocently forget how we started. Life becomes too hostile, and we become so preoccupied with survival that we don't have time to trust our hearts anymore. This happens to most of us in one way or another through hard and sometimes traumatic experiences. Yet within this struggle lies an opportunity for profound healing.

The path back to wholeness requires a shift in perspective: from a mindset of lack and the pursuit of fleeting happiness to one of abundance and inner peace. Often, we operate from a place of scarcity, believing that love, joy, or worthiness are external resources we must earn or chase. This mindset can perpetuate a cycle of striving and dissatisfaction, leading us further away from our true selves. However, when we embrace the abundance already present within us—the inherent worthiness, love, and joy that are our birthright—we begin to cultivate inner peace. It is this peace, not the fleeting highs of happiness, that allows us to reconnect with our hearts and the clean slate of wholeness we were born with.

It might be a big leap to suggest that our struggles with food could help heal this battlefield inside ourselves and restore our trust in giving and receiving love, but that's exactly what I propose. Food-related challenges can help you see if you're running life on a lack or abundance model, if you've learned to be loving to yourself and the places inside of you that hurt, and which parts within you are hurting and need your care. The framework of this care model allows you to "learn as you go" and use everything to assist your learning. Whether you diet or don't diet, whether you count calories or go on a GLP-1 medication, and whether you eat processed foods or give up nightshades, all of it is a guide to discover and forgive self-judgments and false beliefs and to build wisdom, not a sign that you are messing up or losing your moral compass.

Our culture often portrays food challenges as problems to be fixed, demanding significant time and effort. To be clear, embarking on self-compassion requires our attention, commitment, and care; it's simple but only sometimes easy. Leaning into places inside of ourselves that hurt is uncomfortable, but it works. Embracing discomfort through self-compassion is a direct line into life with meaning, connection, and safety. It is an evidence-backed path that is not often taught in our culture. When we practice it, our relationships improve, and that includes the relationship we have with food. We naturally switch from depending on food to help soothe our big feelings to trusting ourselves to soothe those feelings.

A Radical Epiphany
Recently, I had blood work done for a life insurance policy, and my lab results showed that I was just a few clicks shy of prediabetes. Although I consider myself a healthy eater, I had recently added some foods I

didn't usually eat to diversify my diet, stopped exercising as much as I previously had, and adopted an intuitive eating approach. Slowly, the weight crept on, my blood lipids rose, my blood pressure increased, and my body became uncomfortable.

My discomfort had caused me to not socialize in certain situations because of how I perceived myself to look. Some may say that my bigger size was my natural size or that I was buying into diet culture to explain my discomfort. But now that I had lab work that showed I was on my way toward ill health, I was faced with the "what do I do now" question. Lean into self-love and embrace my weight? Tell my doctors that my weight has no bearing on my health? Yes, I could do those things. But something peculiar happened right after I was considering my choices that helped me refocus on how I would deal with this new issue I was facing.

My husband and I were taking a walk, discussing my new health challenges, and he casually said to me, "Well, you do this for a living, so you love your body at any size, and this shouldn't be an issue for you, right?"

I paused for a moment and thought deeply about his question. I decided to be completely honest with him and myself.

"No, I don't love my body. I haven't had one day living in my body that I can say I love it or how I look. I've just found peace with the disappointment that I didn't get the body I would have liked, even though I appreciate my body and all the things it does."

His eyes widened, and he looked at me. "I did not expect to hear you say that."

I continued, "I've decided to focus on making peace with my disappointment instead of trying to force myself into feeling something I'm not—like feeling body positive or accepting. That is an island I've never visited, and truthfully, I think many would agree with me. Our society seems focused on everyone finding happiness with what they have, and I get it. But I haven't been able to do that. Someday, I may experience happiness with my body, but right now, I'm okay with not being okay."

What do you think about choosing peace over happiness? It may seem subtle, but the distinction is profound. Rather than simply accepting my disappointment, I chose to actively engage with the part of me that was deeply unhappy with my body—and in doing so, I found peace. I learned to communicate with that part of myself, offer it care and compassion, and even negotiate with it. This was a radical shift from my previous approach, which involved either trying to suppress those feelings or eliminate them entirely. Embracing cooperation, care, and compassion brought me tremendous freedom, enabling me to support myself unconditionally and empowering me with choice.

When I decided to focus on finding peace with disappointment about my body, an interesting thing happened: I stopped fearing that I was choosing the wrong path and started trusting myself more. This freed me from the worry that actively losing weight after my recent lab work meant buying into diet culture or that not losing weight meant not caring about my health. It also allowed me to experiment and try things, knowing I could support myself wherever I landed. There was no more second-guessing or wondering if I was following the "right" moral code. I could cooperate with my health challenges and create a plan that worked for me, confident that I'd be there for myself with kindness and care, regardless of the outcome.

Yes, I'm writing these words, but I want to acknowledge that this isn't easy. Caring for myself without judgment has never been easy. It feels awkward, clunky, and even a bit forced—definitely not intuitive. Punishing myself with judgment? Easy. Being loving to my hurting parts? Not easy.

Talking to ourselves with kindness takes practice. Here are some of the phrases I said to the parts of me that were disappointed about my natural body and my premenopausal insulin-resistant state:

- "I am so sorry it wasn't different. It's okay to want something else."
- "I know. It is *so* freaking hard to be in a body."
- "This is so confusing. I'm unsure how to care for myself as I undertake a new way of caring for myself, but that's okay. We can be confused together."
- "I am so sorry it seems everyone has it so much easier. Life feels unfair sometimes."
- "You can be mad about this. It's okay."

Facing the lifelong dislike of my body and saying kind words to myself helped me make healthier eating choices and stick to a plan of eating to support my health from a place of abundance rather than lack. It's also helped me be kinder to myself when I don't. Some might say that facing my disappointment isn't abundance, but facing what we feel is truth inside of us and being honest that it's there is how we begin to make peace.

Exercise: Saying Kind Words to the Part of You That's Struggling

Take a minute here to pause. How often do you acknowledge uncomfortable feelings you have? It's a lot like talking to a good friend: Sometimes we call them up and just need to share what we're feeling. They can't do anything about it necessarily, but they can listen, and then we feel better. We can do that for ourselves and the feelings we have, and when we do, it can be healing. Remember, emotional eating is often tied to poor eating choices and the feelings that arise from them, and kindness works better than persecution when we're trying to sort through those feelings. Kind words, more than positive words, help us implement our personal goals.

So, what kind things could you say to yourself right now about how you may be struggling with your body? How does it feel to hear kind words? What do you notice?

The Lack and Abundance Models

Lack is a scarcity orientation that assumes that something is broken and needs fixing, that there isn't enough, that the glass is half empty, that something "bad" is always on the horizon. An abundance orientation toward life is based on the idea that there's enough to go around. It's gratitude for what's present and trust for what's to come. It's a "glass is half full" approach to life. Most of us don't live life from an abundance orientation, including me. But I really thought I did, because I was checking all the boxes that the world told me I should.

Remember earlier in the book when I mentioned how I believed I was unlovable? I thought this until my late thirties, and I had a handy tool kit for trying to compensate for that belief—namely trying to prove I was lovable rather than challenge the belief that I was unlovable. Every move I made was to prove in some way or another that I was lovable, even in my relationship with food. I spent very little time questioning my unlovability. It seems odd now, because I have had a bit of practice questioning my own beliefs. But back then, I didn't. I had my whole life thus far as proof of my unlovability. I was so sure that the anxiety and pain I felt were the indicators of my truth about this, and it felt as though my life fully accommodated this.

In some way, this may be the case for you, too. Of all the core beliefs that impact our relationship with food, some version of "I am unlovable" tends to be present. This deficit fully permeated my life, and I wasn't aware of it in the least until my entire life fell apart because none of my regular coping mechanisms worked anymore.

Now that I've discovered this pattern, when I look back, I see that my first marriage was almost entirely built on this. It looked like a normal relationship—and in many ways, it was—but I had quietly convinced myself that this marriage was right because he was the person who would convince me I was lovable. My marriage was built on a lack inside myself due to the core belief that had been running me for so long that I thought it was the truth and defended it. So then, when my world collapsed and he left me, at first I considered it proof I was unlovable.

Thankfully, I had very wise teachers, and since I had no other tactics for rationalizing and running away from my core beliefs, I stopped running and decided to start trusting. *Before this moment, I set my life around proving I was lovable instead of caring for the part of myself that believed I was unlovable.* That was an important realization—a life-changing one for me. A world-tilting, cosmic-inducing, instant-transformation kind of realization. And more than that, once I saw this framework clearly, I didn't know what to do about it and questioned if I had the internal resources to make a meaningful life change.

I have hundreds of stories and episodes like this—ways I tried to fill the deficit I thought I had—which kept me in a lack model of life instead of an abundance model. I now view lack and abundance models as tools to encourage me to go deeper into my self-compassion and reparenting skills. For example:

My lack orientation: I'm unlovable, but I can prove I'm lovable by how people treat me and love me. If I don't judge how I handle things, I won't have a measure for my value as a person. The world and my accomplishments will show me how well I'm doing. I'll adopt an "us vs. them" model with rules, rigidity, and self-punishment.

My abundance orientation: A part of me feels unlovable because of the big, hard things that happened in my life. I have everything I need to address my needs, even if it's scary to do so. I can soothe and provide that part of myself with the safety it's looking for; I can be loving to the part of me that feels unloved and scorned by the world. I will feel relief if I stop judging how I'm handling things.

Exercise: Do You Identify with Lack or Abundance?

Take a moment to answer these questions:

- Do you feel like your life is supporting you or punishing you? Explain.
- Write about how you live from a lack model and how you live from an abundance model.
- Consider that there may be things you believe about yourself in the lack model that might not be true. What are those things? Is there anything that happened to you that caused you to believe them?

Find and Forgive Your Judgment

When we encounter difficulties, many of us make assumptions about ourselves that aren't true, and we mistakenly label these assumptions as practicality. For example, we sometimes forget that there are practical aspects to eating, such as grocery shopping and deciding what to cook, because once we're in the grocery store and we buy foods we didn't intend to buy, we assume we are weak. Or when we go out to eat with friends and eat more than we intended, we can feel guilt and shame. It can sound something like this: "I'm so mad at myself. I was out with friends and meant to order grilled fish and vegetables, but instead I ordered Fettuccine Alfredo"

I frequently hear from my clients about food challenges that start with a practical element but evolve into self-judgment. Why does this happen? It's challenging to be kind to ourselves, "veering off course" when our natural default is to be critical. Then small things like grocery shopping or eating can become events for which we judge ourselves harshly. Beliefs we mistakenly hold as true can often lead to reflexive judgments and a critical stance when we deviate from our intended path, like only buying things on the grocery list or ordering a healthy dish at a restaurant. The more we practice self-kindness and apply it whenever and wherever needed, the less we fall into self-judgment.

Exercise: How Hard Are You on Yourself?

Read the following statements and decide if each is true or false:

- Finding peace around food is a struggle; I must be doing something wrong because I can't find peace.

- I can't find the strength to resist my urge to binge. Bingeing initially makes me feel better, but afterward, I'm consumed by shame. I feel like a complete failure.
- It feels like everyone in my life abandons me. Food is the only constant in my life. There must be something about me that drives everyone away.
- My health is my responsibility, and I must muster the strength to eat healthy. I have no one to blame if I can't cure my illness, and if I can't, it's proof that I don't deserve a life free from disease.

How many of those statements did you find to be true? Consider that you might be harder on yourself than you need to be. Each of the statements contains an element of self-judgment. How frequently have you engaged in self-deprecation when you've struggled with something?

It's incredibly easy to insert critical views about ourselves into our narratives. It's literally like second nature for humans. Instead, we could choose to eliminate judgment. How can you eliminate your harsh judgments toward yourself? Try the following five steps:

1. Be honest about your judgments. Write them down.
2. Practice being open toward yourself about having them.
3. Try saying a kind thing to yourself multiple times a day.
4. Realize that the more untrue things you believe about yourself, the more you prime the pump for self-judgment.
5. Work with a practitioner who has been trained to help you understand your beliefs around food, eating, and personal values.

Why Do We Judge Ourselves So Much?

We live in a world where self-criticism is pervasive. Often, with food, we use it as a tool to label ourselves harshly, express self-disdain, or compensate for perceived shortcomings. Achieving peace around food can indeed be a challenge. But we humans don't just leave it at that; we delve further and make assumptions that compound these challenging experiences. Society reinforces this. We carry more than just practical challenges when it comes to food; we go a step further and decide if we are the source of the problem or, even worse, the problem itself. Why do we judge ourselves? *It is the easiest way to make challenges add up in our minds and hearts and to mitigate emotional pain.* Read that last sentence again. It's important. But, remember, challenges with food can help guide us to love the parts that hurt.

We need to distinguish between impractical and practical thinking and understand that we have behaviors that complicate things and behaviors that simplify them. If we don't shop for groceries, we won't have food. If we don't eat, our bodies won't have fuel.

Once you understand that these metaphorical wires often get crossed within you, you can identify and resolve them through self-compassion. These internal crossed wires not only shape your relationship with food, but they also represent the root cause you've been seeking. Remember, you have an internal tool kit capable of inducing a "change of heart" rather than simply a "change of mind."

Chapter Takeaways
- Most of us operate on lack, not abundance, and we don't realize it.
- In general, humans falsely believe they will reach more personal goals by being hard on themselves than by being kind to themselves.
- Focusing on peace instead of happiness about our bodies and our lives is a compassion-based approach that works.
- The very issues we feel we need to battle, cure, and fix are the doorways to our inner parts that believe something about us that isn't true.
- Struggles with food are a direct line between ourselves and the hurting places we can care for—and heal.
- Why do we judge ourselves? Because it's the easiest way to make challenges add up in our minds and hearts and to mitigate emotional pain.
- The heart is stronger than any untrue thing we believe about ourselves.

Chapter 9

Placing the Loving

The spiritual journey is not a career or a success story. It is a series of small humiliations of the false self that become more and more profound. —Carl Jung

I've discussed how self-compassion is an effective tool for building emotional resilience and how reparenting can extend that compassion across our lifetime to restore care and connection to the parts of us that didn't get their emotional needs met. These are the same parts that try to manage our eating with limited resources, often relying on harsh judgments and untrue beliefs to create change. This keeps us stuck in a difficult cycle to break. You've probably grasped this concept by now and hopefully even practiced extending kindness to yourself.

This chapter is special to me, because it will introduce you to an exercise I created that combines self-compassion (self-kindness) and reparenting (traveling your timeline to implement care), but with a revolutionary twist—connecting with the version of yourself that existed *before* life's challenges altered your relationship with food and body.

Why would we do this? Imagine going through some of life's hardest challenges with loving support and not feeling alone. Or reaching back through time to stand beside your younger self before that critical moment when food became complicated, when body image became painful, or when eating became your primary coping mechanism. Being on a GLP-1 medication adds in an extra benefit: It gives space to rewrite the emotional patterns that preceded your food struggles, addressing the root cause rather than just managing symptoms. This process will also be beneficial for your post-GLP-1 life as well, because it builds the inner resilience that you may need for any bumps ahead, food noise, fears about regressing, or weight gain, so you don't fall into old belief patterns that will make that process more challenging.

When we provide loving presence *before* difficult events, we prevent those fragile parts of ourselves from forming the painful, untrue conclusions that have driven emotional eating for years. Instead of trying to heal after the wound forms, we're creating a protective shield of compassion that *changes how the experience is processed from the beginning.* In essence, you prevent an untrue belief from forming by time traveling before a hard event to give yourself support, strength, and safety. This reduces the exhausting work of constantly managing food behaviors that were simply compensating for perceived inadequacies—a pattern I've witnessed in countless clients.

I especially like the lessons of this chapter because they don't directly address the traumatic event itself, making it accessible and safe for those with challenging histories who might hesitate to try self-compassion and reparenting practices. Remember, the core issues blocking you can be transformed through reconnection with your loving self, and that reconnection can happen before, during, or after life's challenges. Trauma disconnects us from inner trust, but the heart is the most effective tool we have to reconnect ourselves to it.

One Event, Two Nervous System Responses
Consider this fictional story: Best friends Morgan and Sarah are sitting together on an airplane, headed for a weekend in Mexico. An hour into the flight, the plane suddenly starts to shake, and an engine goes out. The plane begins a rapid descent, and everyone is wondering if it's going to crash. Panic fills the air and people start screaming. The pilot gets on the intercom and tells everyone that there is a mechanical problem, and they are going to make an emergency landing at the closest airport.

Months after the emergency landing, Sarah and Morgan are still trying to find effective ways of coping with the difficult event they both experienced with their different nervous systems. Sarah has had a relapse of her eating disorder and is experiencing PTSD symptoms. Morgan also experienced some PTSD-like symptoms after the incident, but she got help. She is now writing a book about her experience and has found new meaning in her life through the ordeal—speaking about it publicly, sharing her story of resilience. She was challenged, yes, but not like Sarah, who has struggled much more emotionally.

The two women shared an identical challenging experience, so why the difference? The answer lies in the level of emotional resilience of each before the challenging experience, which impacted how their nervous systems reacted and, more important, recovered. Morgan had been provided a safe, stable, and loving environment growing up; Sarah had not, and she hadn't built any for herself as an adult.

As I've shared in this book, building up emotional resilience is possible—through various forms of therapy, practicing self-compassion, and reparenting—but it takes practice, and it takes a vote for yourself. A vote. For yourself. Have you ever consciously done that? You can turn the tide right now. Say it out loud: *I vote for myself.* Today, I choose to vote for myself and take the caring, loving action, even if it feels scary or unfamiliar.

You can learn to give yourself emotional resilience by being a loving, caring, safe presence for yourself even if the event is in the past. Your own care and love can cross space and time and be placed anywhere, anytime.

Eventually, Sarah learned how to give herself love, trust, and safety by practicing the "Placing the Loving" exercise in this chapter for the more challenging events she had experienced. Each time she did, she increased her emotional resilience by being present and loving for herself. She worked through her timeline, eventually ready to work with the plane incident. She imagined giving herself a powerful, loving connection, reassuring herself that even though she would be going through a very challenging event, she wouldn't be alone, hadn't done anything wrong, and was loved. This story about Morgan and Sarah illustrates the power we all hold for healing. We can shift our focus from fixing trauma to providing emotional safety, and we have the option to do this by offering ourselves our own loving presence.

Jenny's Story

Jenny, a happily married mother to three children, came to see me after a recent diagnosis of Type 2 diabetes. Along with her doctor she was focused on finding the best blend of medications, supplements, and diet she could use to reverse it . She was overwhelmed by trying to find someone who could help her, so she hopped from protocol to protocol and became exhausted trying to find the "right" answers and the most appropriate plan for her needs.

When discussing her current feelings about how to navigate her current health journey and find the best food plan to support her body's healing, she revealed to me that it felt like her nervous system was in a fight-or-flight response all the time. She didn't know how to distinguish good information from bad, and that stemmed from her childhood. Her parents divorced when she was six, and she immediately felt like a pawn between them and didn't know who she could trust or believe.

The divorce was preceded by her siblings bullying and teasing her for her weight. Because her parents were preoccupied with their divorce drama and Jenny was the youngest child, her older siblings cared for her and prepared her meals. She was continually teased for being overweight, which was a result of using food to comfort and provide solace for herself. She often felt terrified growing up, not knowing who was friend or foe in her family. One minute, her siblings were fun and nice, and the next, they were harsh and cruel. Her parents did not step in to help Jenny navigate this sibling dynamic, because they were too overwhelmed with their own issues.

In her twenties, Jenny found WeightWatchers and lost a significant amount of weight. She finally felt in control of her body and life. She found a beloved community in her local group and flourished during that process. Years later, married and still having kept the weight off, she felt that all her body issues were behind her. After her type-2 diabetes diagnosis, she wanted a solid plan like WeightWatchers to support her health but also to help her find the comfort and safety she craved after experiencing out-of-control feelings from her diagnosis.

When we spent time together, I listened to her closely. I heard Jenny say multiple times that she did not know who was a friend or enemy in her family—that she didn't trust herself to know—and that now, in her current state, she was right back in that place she was as a child: searching for those who would not betray her. She felt exhausted, overwhelmed, and resentful. After she had done so much inner work, life was handing her a crap sandwich with a diabetes diagnosis, and all of her coping mechanisms were falling short.

I gently pointed out to Jenny that, growing up, she couldn't trust anyone in her family. Siblings would be nice to her for a while, then turn on her and say cruel things that would be hard to experience as a child. I asked if she thought it was hard to trust others after her parents' divorce, and she said yes. She didn't know who was safe in her family.

"So, growing up, you were confused about who you could trust," I said. "Do you think you trust yourself now?"

"I don't know," she said. "I think I do. But I feel guilty a lot, like I'm missing the right answers about my health, so maybe I don't trust myself."

"Here you are navigating the best healing path for your diabetes, but if you don't trust yourself, then do you think that would make it hard to know the best path, forcing you to look outside yourself to find the 'right' answers?"

"Wow, I hadn't thought about that before," Jenny said. "Yes, it makes sense. I was so young and confused, I didn't know the right path when I was younger. I guess I do still feel like that when I lean into it now talking to you. I mean, I feel a sense of calm talking about that, but I also feel sad. I was just a little girl, often feeling alone and wishing someone would care for and comfort me. I had no one to help me."

As a practitioner helping Jenny understand her core beliefs, I realized that she had an "I can't trust myself" core belief. Was it true she couldn't trust herself? No. However, as a child, she had no caring person who intervened to clear up that misconception, and she was doing her best with what she had. "I can't trust myself" became the bad data that created an entire reality system in her life. It became an unconscious safety pattern that persisted to this day and is still informing her relationship with food.

When she couldn't trust herself, her inward instincts became unreliable, so she had to become skilled at finding trust outside of herself. Food and bingeing helped her feel calm from the chaos of not knowing who and what to trust. But now that she was faced with a bigger challenge than she had previously experienced, her coping mechanism of being hypervigilant in finding a unicorn practitioner or diet to do the trusting for her was not working, and she was panicking. Her core belief would block her from finding the connection inside herself to trust the answers from doctors and practitioners. Also, it would likely keep showing up as a repeating "problem," engaging with her as a life pattern to help her clear it up.

She was being given an opportunity to address this bad data core belief through her journey with diabetes. She thought it was life punishing her. Yes, it was scary and big, but it was also a chance to love and care for herself in a way she hadn't yet. She had to trust that her love and care would be enough for her younger self, who was still back in time, frozen in place because she didn't know who she could trust. She always thought her "savior" would be someone she found with all the wisdom and care, but the only person who could do the work of rescuing her younger self was her current self.

I think it would be helpful to read a transcript of one of our sessions, so you can clearly see how the process can work.

Me: Would you imagine for a moment that you're standing next to your younger self? How is her nervous system? Is it dysregulated?

Jenny: Yes, her nervous system is a wreck. She's terrified.

Me: You can regulate her nervous system with deep care, presence, and connection. Would you like to do that?

Jenny: Oh my gosh, yes!

Me: Could I take you through a reparenting process, Jenny? It's called "Placing the Loving."

Jenny: Sure.

Me: Choose a time you remember being dysregulated or upset as a little girl. Tell me what event you choose.

Jenny: It was my seventh birthday party. I was so excited and happy, but at my party, surrounded by my entire family, my sister told me that if I ate a big piece of cake, I would turn into a fatso. I never overcame that day's shame, anger, and embarrassment.

Me: Okay, sounds good. Let's get started. Since you're already sitting and in a comfortable position, just close your eyes and listen to my voice. Only do what feels safe and comfortable. Take a few deep breaths and imagine you're walking down a hallway. At the end of the hallway is a door, and behind that door is little you before her birthday party. From this point forward, I'll refer to you as "big you" (the current you) and "little you" (the younger part you will visit). Okay, let me know what you see.

Jenny: I walk into my room. I'm getting ready for my party. I have a brand-new dress I will wear laid out on the bed. I'm bursting with happiness. I got the special Oreo cookie ice-cream cake from Baskin-Robbins, and my three next-door neighbor friends are coming with my family.

Me: Perfect. Walk over to little you and ask if you can visit her before the party.

Jenny: Okay. She said yes.

Me: Great. Sit down on the bed with her and tell her how happy you are to see her.

Jenny: Okay. I'm sitting on the bed, and she wonders why I'm there but is happy to see me, too. She recognizes me.

Me: Ask her if it's okay to hold her hand.

Jenny: She says yes. I'm holding her hand now.

Me: Look her in the eyes and tell her you've come to visit her to give her a gift.

Jenny: Oh, she loves that. She's excited.

Me: Tell her that she's going to be doing a hard thing but tell her it will be okay. Tell her you will be with her the whole time, and she won't be alone. Tell her she hasn't done anything wrong to cause this hard thing to happen, and tell her you are sorry it has to be this way.

Jenny: Okay, I told her. She's looking at me intently.

Me: Hold out your hand and see a grain of sand. Imagine filling the grain of sand with unconditional love for the little you. See it as bright, wondrous light that grows and grows. See it grow as big as a basketball. See this glowing ball of love for her lighting up the room, light reflecting off your face. When the grain of sand is filled and the size of a basketball, I want you to tell her: "This is for you so that you can remember you will never be alone and that I will be with you the whole way. You haven't done anything wrong, and I love you so much. I am so sorry you have to do this, but you will be okay. We are going to do it together."

Jenny: Okay, I told her everything.

Me: Perfect. Now, give her the big ball of love. See her put it in her heart. Take a deep breath and let me know how she feels once she receives this gift. How does she feel in her body and heart?

Jenny: I just gave it to her, and she put it in her heart. She feels different, like stronger or something. She feels safe and connected to me.

Me: That's wonderful. Now, you have some choices. You can ask little you if she wants to come back with you and live where you currently live, or if it's okay, go with her to the birthday party, or if you can leave and come back to see her very soon. (it's just adding "or" after currently live). Give her the options and let me know what she says.

Jenny: She wants me to go to the party with her.

Me: Okay. Are you up for that?

Jenny: Absolutely.

Me: Great. Have little you lead the way.

Jenny: Okay, I helped dress her and tie her hair in a bow. It was really sweet. We're walking hand in hand into the dining room where my party and cake are. All of my brothers and sisters are there.

Me: Perfect. So, imagine that no one notices your presence.

Jenny: Okay. I got it. She's sitting down at the table, and everyone is around her. They are about to light the candles and sing "Happy Birthday." I pull up a chair and sit next to her.

Me: Okay, perfect. Take her hand and remind her that you're not going anywhere, and she hasn't done anything wrong. Tell her how happy you are to be with her at her party, and there is nowhere else you'd rather be than celebrating her. As you both sit there, see the ball of love you gave to her back in her room. Notice how it connects her differently to you, the person with complete, unconditional love for her.

Jenny: Okay, I'm squeezing her hand and beaming with love for her. My family and my three friends sing the "Happy Birthday" song. My older sister cuts the cake and starts passing out pieces. She hands her a plate with a very small piece of cake and says in front of everyone that she should only eat a few bites, so she won't turn into a bigger fatso. Everyone starts laughing.

Me: Look at little you and tell her how sorry you are that your sister said that, and you are there with her and she hasn't done anything wrong. Let her know you aren't going anywhere, and she isn't alone.

Jenny: Okay, yes. Seeing how that comment cut so deep in her is so sad. I'm squeezing her hand, looking into her eyes, and letting her know there is no place I'd rather be than with her. I'm telling her how much I love her, she isn't alone, I'm not leaving, and she didn't do anything wrong.

Me: Great. Notice how she feels in her body with you saying that.

Jenny: She's upset, but it's not as bad as I remember it.

Me: Good. Ask her if she needs anything else.

Jenny: Okay, she asked if she could get a hug, and I gave her one. I also asked her if she wants to sit in my lap.

Me: Wonderful. Now, notice how she feels in her body when you care for her, love her, and help her feel safe. What do you notice?

Jenny: She's still upset but feels protected and safe now. She feels less dejected. She keeps squeezing my hand, and I keep telling her what a great job she's doing.

Me: Yes. Now, ask her if she'd like to come home and live with you.

Jenny: Yes. She wants to be with me.

Me: Okay, scoop her up and tell her she gets to live with you, and you will never leave her. Start walking out of the room and see yourself carrying her down a hallway. At the end, there is a door. When you walk through the door, see yourself walking back into the room you are sitting in now. Sit down, both of you, and give her a big hug. Ask her if there's anything she needs right now.

Jenny: She said a big piece of birthday cake from Baskin-Robbins and me sitting next to her.

Me: Fantastic. Imagine yourself giving her a piece of cake. Put a candle in it if you want—whatever feels right. Tell her how happy you are to be with her now and how you will care for her.

Jenny (softly weeping): Yes, we are together, and we both feel so much better.

Through the "Placing The Loving" reparenting exercise, Jenny was able to address her core belief of "I can't trust myself" by providing emotional safety for herself through comforting and connecting with her younger self. Doing this over time changed the core belief. While her lifestyle changes remained a work in progress, the breakthrough was profound. She was able to shift away from viewing her diabetes management with a pass/fail mindset focused on perfection. Instead she developed greater resilience that gave her confidence to explore and find her own path for healing. The newfound self-trust meant she no longer felt desperate to find the "right" answer from external sources or placed overwhelming pressure on herself to be perfect, but rather felt empowered to navigate her healing journey with patience and self-compassion.

Exercise: "Placing the Loving" Meditation

In Jenny's story, I walked her through this meditation. It's one of the exercises I use most in my professional practice and in my classes. I love it because it doesn't go straight into a traumatic event—it goes before it, which is wonderful for highly traumatized people or those who emotionally dysregulate easily. The goal of this exercise is to provide safety, compassion, and resilience for yourself before a challenging event, so that when you relive the event (even though it has already happened), you have more resources available to you and are less likely to create illusions or false beliefs about yourself. (If you'd like to listen to this meditation, you can do so here: insighttimer.com/thelovingdiet/guided-meditations/placing-the-loving.)

To practice this meditation, pick an event that was challenging for you, but not too challenging (at least at first). Intend to visit younger you before the challenging event happened. Center yourself with a few breaths, connecting with your physical heart and then your compassionate heart or inner loving self. Then begin the meditation:

Imagine yourself inside your compassionate heart, seeing a doorway you will walk through.

See yourself walking down a hallway to visit younger you.

Visualize walking into a room or scene where younger you lives—before the hard event happened.

Walk up to younger you and tell them you came to visit and to give them a gift.

Let them know they are going to be doing a hard thing, but you will be with them the whole time.

Let them know they haven't done anything wrong, and you are so sorry it has to be this way.

Tell them you came to visit them to give the gift of knowing they aren't alone and won't be alone, because you will be with them the whole time.

Hold out your hand and see a grain of sand. Fill the grain of sand with the feeling and energy of deep love and care for younger you and what they are going to be going through.

See the grain of sand grow to a large ball of love, the size of a basketball.

Give the ball of love to younger you, telling them, "This is for you, so you don't ever forget you will never be alone and I love you."

See younger you put the ball of love into their heart.

Pause for moment. How does younger you feel putting the ball of love into their heart?

What are you both feeling and experiencing?

Tell younger you they can come back with you or stay there and that there are no wrong answers. If they want to stay there, let them know you will be back to visit them. If they'd like to come back with you, hold their hand and lead them out of the room, down the hallway, and back into the room you are in. If you are leaving them in the room, visualize walking back down the hallway and into the room you are currently in.

Ask them if they need anything as you get them comfortable in their new surroundings.

Take a moment to reflect on this exercise and experience. How do you feel? What are you experiencing? Write about it in your journal.

* * *

"Placing the Loving" is one of the most effective ways to incorporate the best parts of self-compassion and reparenting. It's especially beneficial for those hesitant to start or lacking access to a skilled therapist. This exercise doesn't take you directly into the challenging event, which can be destabilizing for some. Instead, it connects you with your younger self *before* a challenge, gifting them with compassion-based resources and allowing them to experience the challenge with more emotional resources.

Know that, energetically, "Placing the Loving" allows you to connect with the version of yourself that doesn't have a dysregulated nervous system. This circumvents the need to focus on regulating your nervous system to heal and extends tools of resilience for going through a challenge. The exercise builds inner strength effectively, prevents false beliefs from forming, and regulates your nervous system before facing a challenge, yet it is so gentle you can use it repeatedly, even for the same event.

Chapter Takeaways
- Trauma disconnects us from inner trust, but the heart is the most effective tool we have to reconnect ourselves to it.
- If you have core issues that are blocking growth, you can solve them by reconnecting with your loving self, and that reconnection can happen before, during, or after a challenge.
- By visiting yourself *before* a challenging event, you can remind yourself that you will be okay and will have everything you need to survive it.
- You can't change what happened to you, but with the power of your heart, you can change what you decided about yourself as a result.
- Love isn't bound by space and time, so it can be used to remind younger parts of yourself that they aren't alone and that they are safe and loved.
- Moving your own love up and down your timeline builds emotional resilience and regulates the nervous system of today.
- "Placing the Loving" is a great exercise for those who do not want to go back into the memories of a traumatic event.

Chapter 10

Is Your Past Pushing You Forward or Your Future Pulling You to It?

The mystic is not somebody who says, "Look what I've experienced. Look what I've achieved." The mystic is the one who says, "Look what love has done to me." ... There's nothing left, but the being of love itself giving itself away as ... the concreteness of who you simply are.
—James Finley

Your relationship with GLP-1 medication marks more than a medical intervention; it's an invitation to see how you relate to yourself and your life differently. For too long, troubled relationships with food, your body, and life itself defined how you told your story, rooted in wounds you didn't create but carried nonetheless. These struggles have pushed you forward from behind, perhaps feeling like shadows you can't outrun. But what if this journey you're on offers a way to end that cycle? Not just with weight management, but with a pivotal moment to change directions and be pulled forward by possibility rather than pushed by pain. Do you identify more with the burdens of your past or the unwritten possibilities of your future?

In this chapter, we'll explore *how* to shift your eating-based orientation from the past to the future, examining the belief frameworks that may be holding you back. My work has shown that many of us use past experiences as a driving force, and we don't even realize it. However, if your past has been challenging, this approach may be rooted in a sense of brokenness rather than striving toward your full potential. Now that we've learned how to practice "Placing the Loving" on past events, it's time to uncover your untapped future and develop a daily practice to harness the transformative power of your heart—a love so powerful it can transcend time to heal past wounds by identifying with your healed and whole future self.

The Path of Peace

If pain and struggle mark a difficult relationship with food and eating, wouldn't happiness and joy signify a healed one? It seems logical, but I've come to believe otherwise. I once thought that finding my healing "nirvana" would bring lasting happiness. For a moment, it did. However, that joy, tied to an unsustainable surge of feel-good chemicals, quickly faded. Ever reach your goal weight on a fad diet and feel really good for a few days only to find yourself back in your old thought patterns of tearing yourself down? We often think "Once I reach my goal weight, then I can start living my life" or "Once I reach my goal weight then I'll be happy." We relentlessly chase happiness as a marker of success, yet it remains a perpetually fleeting sensation.

Instead, I encourage you to pursue peace with food and your body as the desired state for your future self. Achievable and enduring, peace is far more potent and encompassing than fleeting happiness. It arises naturally when you refrain from self-judgment and treat all parts of yourself—even the ones you dislike—with respect and gratitude.

Finding peace with our bodies by focusing on the possibility that our future selves hold relies on trusting our lives, vulnerability, and practice. I type that out like it's easy, but it's not, because with peace can come disappointment, which most of us avoid at all costs. To find lasting peace with food and your body on your GLP-1 journey, you're required to face the disappointment that body perfection isn't a realistic goal for humans, because it simply doesn't exist. When you acknowledge that, you find peace.

Most of us focus on our past as a default instead of our future selves. How do I know this? One glimpse at any bookstore, podcast list, or social media influencer's account shows us that we are a world indoctrinated into the cult of "self-improvement," which is firmly rooted in the idea that we aren't good enough as we are. Hard work isn't wrong, but working hard to prove our goodness is an example of the rampant self-improvement illusion that has saturated the healing world.

If you recognize and cherish your wholeness and accept disappointment as part of the human experience, peace can transform your relationship with yourself, food, and your body. Simply put, the less you judge yourself for your eating behaviors, the more peace you'll experience and the healthier your relationship with food becomes.

To free ourselves from the judgment around food and body image, we can consider something different: transcending the pass/fail and happy/suffering duality. This requires building a new framework, one that replaces the belief "If I emotionally eat, I am failing" with "If I emotionally eat, I am not a failure." This shift demands identifying the parts of ourselves that have internalized the label of "failure" and using self-compassion to rewrite that narrative.

Jackie's Story

In one of our sessions, my client Jackie shared how hard it was living with fibromyalgia and type-2 diabetes. She'd seen dozens of doctors over the years, trying to find relief for her pain and fatigue, which had themselves resulted in a loss of mobility and unwanted weight gain.

In the last few years, she'd been drawn to the idea of "treating the root cause" promised by functional medicine. What she found instead was a string of mostly thin, male doctors who told her the key to healing naturally relied largely on her mindset and willpower, along with a lengthy list of supplements, a very low carbohydrate diet, and regular, vigorous exercise. But her fatigue and chronic pain didn't lessen and prevented her from being able to follow through on the recommendations and protocols. She was left believing that she was the problem, rather than the unrealistic protocols her largely out-of-touch male doctors had given her.

The belief that she was the problem had solidified over many years, beginning in childhood. Jackie had grown up being forced to eat everything on her plate, and when she couldn't, she was labeled as picky, problematic, and a failure. She had endured years of merciless shaming from a stepparent who had made her feel that she was a challenging, troubled soul.

Jackie had never revisited or reevaluated this central belief, and it had unconsciously haunted her in different ways for years. The belief that began as "I am a problematic, picky eater" in her early years had eventually morphed into "I'm a problem, and it's my fault that I'm not well." Now it hung over her (largely unnoticed) as an adult trying her best to care for her condition. As a result, her limiting belief had become tightly wound into good intentions to help herself find solutions to her chronic health condition. Those good intentions sounded something like what our culture loves to promote: Follow your intuition for self-improvement. To self-improve, she would have to fix her problem; that is, it was her fault she wasn't well. Once she did that, she would be able to follow through and take the long list of supplements and follow the vigorous exercise plan... and then she would be healed.

I suggested she approach the "problem" from a different starting point: looking at the deep-seated belief informing her intuition that she thought was true but wasn't. By engaging her heart, Jackie could implement a better-functioning intuition to help her navigate her health journey. This approach would allow her to stop fixing her "brokenness," which is a lack perspective, and instead engage in a healing approach from an abundance perspective where she wasn't the problem. But to do this she would need to address how she continually created her future path with her old false beliefs still running the show.

I asked her to identify the stuck place she found herself in. "I can't get better because I believe I am the problem," she said. So, we started there and looked at it dynamically: from the past, present, and future.

Exercise: Past, Present, and Future

Here's the exercise I did with Jackie, which is designed to help you work with a false belief from the past, present, and future to transform it. I'm using her as an example, but you can try it for your own challenges, as it's an effective way to work from a solution-oriented place rather than a fixing place. Just start with the first thing that comes to mind when you ask yourself what you believe is your main issue. Write it down.

Now, look at the issue in three different ways:

1. **In the present:** Forgive yourself for what you believe today.
2. **In the past:** Reparent the part of you that, to stay safe, decided that belief in the first place.
3. **In the future:** Identify with the whole part of you that has worked through this in the future.

Let's look at how Jackie practiced this exercise. (I'm again using a transcript from one of our sessions to help illustrate the process for you.)

In the Present

Jackie believed that she couldn't get better because she was the problem. I asked her to forgive herself for believing this.

Me: Just repeat after me: "I forgive myself for believing I can't get better because I am the problem."

Jackie repeated the statement.

Me: Great. Now take a deep breath. What are you experiencing right now?

Jackie: I feel so much sadness. I have felt this for so long.

Me: Do you feel like you have judged yourself for believing this?

Jackie: Yes.

Me: Okay, then repeat after me: "I forgive myself *for judging myself* for believing I can't get better because I am the problem."

Jackie repeated the statement.

Me: Take a deep breath. What are you experiencing now?

Jackie: I feel better. Lighter, calmer, but sad.

Jackie's homework was to repeat these forgiveness statements whenever the belief or stuck feeling returned.

In the Past

We then worked on the "Give Yourself What You Didn't Receive" exercise in Chapter 7. Remember, the key is to connect with the part of yourself that holds the belief, recognizing it was formed innocently as a coping mechanism. Imagine visiting your younger self and reassuring them that:

1. They didn't do anything wrong.
2. They aren't alone.
3. You are sorry it had to be that way.

Offer your younger self the option to come live with you in the present, or say goodbye and promise to return. Love and connection heal false beliefs. Jackie's younger self held a story that she was a problem. That story like many fictional accounts can, over time, come to feel true, because we revisit it so often in our mind, replaying it over and over. On top of that, humans have a really bad habit of making themselves the villain or victim, instead of recognizing they were just doing the best they could with what they had. Jackie's picky eating that developed over time was both soothing balm for the yelling in the house and for the part of her convinced it was somehow her fault it was happening. Often when we eat, that is the only break we get from that narrative. Fast forward to the present day when she consciously wants to eat for her health; it won't seem natural to stray from her old eating habits until she clears up the untrue story driving her eating patterns that set her relationship with food into motion. By taking the time to complete this exercise, Jackie learned how deep her beliefs went and how the lack of willpower wasn't the issue—it was understanding the story she wrote for herself that made sense as a child but is no longer needed as an adult.

In the Future

Finally, Jackie and I focused on identifying with a future version of herself—wise, connected, and free from the limiting belief. This creates a felt sense in the body to identify with, instead of pain from the past. We also used solution-focused questions:

- How would I feel different right now if I allowed myself to consider that my future may be better than I could imagine it to be?
- When I take the time to really visualize this, what does my wise, healed, and connected future self look like? Feel like? Sound like?
- What is holding me back from trusting my life right now?
- What feeling would I experience right now if my life and my body were completely on track, and I wasn't missing anything?

These questions helped Jackie learn to live in the present and allow the future to pull her forward with intent, curiosity, and vulnerability. Prior to this she was defining herself from the past experiences. In a way, she was rewriting history for herself through this exercise and *feeling* how it felt to be living in a body that was wise, connected, and not missing anything. *She shifted the central viewpoint she defined her life by.* Instead of the endless, exhausting search from fixing "I am the problem," she allowed and imagined her whole, healed self, finding and comforting that hurt part that held that untrue belief. Honestly, that is the hardest thing for us humans to do. We can't fathom not being broken. We can't imagine tapping into a vision of ourselves as complete or whole—regardless of our physical health or diagnosis. But Jackie allowed herself to be vulnerable enough to do just this. Not in a boisterous, ego sort of way, but in a childlike wonder sort of way. After all those years of verbal abuse from her stepparent and bullying from others, none of it took away from her inner goodness, and this exercise helped her remember that. It can do the same for you.

Like Jackie, you can use all three steps in one session, or you can spread them out. Either way, the exercise prompts you to work through your belief system with kindness, vulnerability, patience, and appreciation. When you approach untrue beliefs with love, you heal. Remember, love is the most effective path for healing from the false narratives we create for safety, which can ultimately hinder our growth.

* * *

Taking the time to discover if your belief system is rooted in the past, present, or future is a way to meet your goals in a new way. While we've talked about various ways to understand how to compassionately work with parts, discover beliefs, and take off Life Jackets, this approach allows you the freedom and expression to imagine your future "better than you thought it could be" by imagining a whole, healed you drawing you toward it, rather than a past you are trying to put behind you. This makes it much easier to make that vision a reality and find lasting peace with food and your body.

Chapter Takeaways

- Your GLP-1 journey offers you a pivotal moment to change directions and be pulled forward by possibility rather than pushed by pain.
- You can harness the transformative power of your heart—a love so powerful it can transcend time to heal past wounds by identifying with your healed and whole future self.
- Happiness is elusive and fleeting. Peace is transformative and achievable.
- The less you judge yourself for your eating behaviors, the more peace you'll experience and the healthier your relationship with food becomes.
- Remember, love is the most effective path for healing from the false narratives we create for safety, which can ultimately hinder our growth.

- Love and compassion in our heart can transcend space and time and can change a limiting belief, because love is just as strong as beliefs put in place for emotional safety.
- You can learn how to change a belief by working with the past, present, and future.
- Past beliefs can be touched with compassion through reparenting techniques; present beliefs can be forgiven in real time; and future whole selves can be called upon to provide a felt sense of safety, connection, and compassion.

Chapter 11

The Allure of Bypassing Pain

All great spirituality is about what we do with our pain. If we do not transform our pain, we will transmit it to those around us.
—Richard Rohr

In previous chapters, we discovered that using food as a coping mechanism is largely driven by internalized false beliefs of unworthiness. These beliefs, formed in response to challenging experiences, can manifest as Life Jackets—protective strategies that shield us from emotional pain. However, these Life Jackets can also hinder our growth and well-being if we continue to wear them after the crisis has passed.

GLP-1 medications can quiet food noise in a way that feels like a gift – and it is. But that relief can also make it tempting to skip over the deeper work. I want to gently encourage you to use this moment not to bypass your history, but to finally explore it with care and compassion.

Shame, the toxic self-blame often associated with emotional eating, further complicates the healing process. It poisons the soil of compassion, making self-kindness and reparenting feel unattainable, despite their necessity for recovery. It's undeniably difficult to nurture ourselves with self-compassion when we've never experienced it firsthand.

Throughout this book, I've provided a road map, guiding you into your heart with meditations, visualizations, questions, and exercises. In this chapter, we'll examine how the spiritual self-improvement strategies gaining popularity, which emphasize the mind-body connection, can be effective but can also inadvertently lead to emotional or spiritual bypassing—the use of practices, approaches, or beliefs to avoid difficult emotions rather than genuinely addressing them. And here's the truth: If our relationship with food doesn't lead us to correct our false beliefs and love ourselves, some other challenge in our lives will appear to help us heal, grow, and learn to love ourselves.

Blurring Lines in Healing Movements

The lines between traditional and alternative healing methods are blurring. Therapists are incorporating shamanic practices, personal trainers are delving into clients' Akashic records, and nutritionists are teaching trauma healing through somatic exercises. It's a diverse healing buffet, and some would say it's a good time to be alive, because the world is becoming more open-minded about different approaches to healing.

The same is true in the world of eating: Rigid rules are being replaced with a no-rules approach to nourishment. This newfound freedom is comforting, but there's a downside when we use these methods to turn our backs on science, practicality, and kindness. It's a nuanced path to take a nugget of wisdom about health from a person channeling the Galactic Council while also remembering to get our cholesterol checked yearly. Humans often prefer the easy path, avoiding the painful places within themselves. It's easier to unconsciously defend our untrue beliefs than to face the discomfort of changing them or the embarrassment of having believed them in the first place.

In our quest to trust our heart, we must confront how our pursuit of emotional comfort can lead us to disregard challenging emotions that need addressing. Emotional eating is a prime example of using alternative healing as a shield against facing difficult realities. I often see this in my practice with clients attempting to practice intuitive eating while struggling with emotional eating. They lean into their intuition for unconditional permission to eat, but the lines become blurred between true hunger and emotional hunger. The burden of untrue beliefs can cloud their intuition, making it hard to distinguish fact from fiction. This is the biggest challenge I see with those trying to eat mindfully or intuitively.

Bypassing—or skirting emotional pain—is a pastime of our culture, and unfortunately, it has saturated the world of emotional eating. Understandably, humans don't want to reconcile pain of any kind. We will do anything to avoid feeling uncomfortable, especially if we think it's optional. Although logically, we know emotional eating is uncomfortable and often destructive, for many, it's more comfortable than facing intense internal suffering head-on. Because of this, we rely on "self-improvement," the promising path that will put distance between us and the scary dark place inside where our suffering lives.

Self-improvement has many names and messages now, like upleveling, 5D ascension, spiritual oracle, or raising your vibration, and many are promising to heal trauma, protect our auras, or improve anything that ails us—including emotional eating. But is it really that simple? In a way, suffering stems from the mistaken belief that we are separate from our innate goodness. But for us more earthly beings working that concept out, the idea of "just choosing" self-improvement can be an oversimplification that does a disservice to the effort required to care for ourselves deeply.

I don't see most of us being able to snap a finger to remove internalized false beliefs, although I humbly admit that I have spent many hours and days wishing it were that easy. Caring for ourselves from a heart-centered place to heal our relationship with food takes time, patience, practice, and a conscious decision to trust ourselves. And as I've mentioned, it takes a commitment to lasting peace, rather than chasing elusive happiness.

It's alluring to consider that our inner work can be done for us by anything other than ourselves. It can't. I see this right now in the GLP-1 movement and in some approaches using psychedelics as a "cure-all" for addictions or traumas. Nothing replaces doing the inner work, even though all the tools coming forward will help with the journey. They can assist, but nothing outside of our heart can change what our heart believes.

Maybe these days you're hearing "eat anything you want" and "embrace your fatness," and you may have found a way to erase the food noise that will cure emotional eating effectively. Being on a GLP-1 medication can radically change how you process those messages. You don't think about food like you used to; you don't struggle with the same issues. That is truly an accomplishment, so don't discount that. But no medication is powerful enough to change or erase the belief system about your innate value or lovability that your relationship with food was compensating for. Only your heart can do that.

Reconciling with your cast-out parts and loving them is hard work, can't be bypassed, and is perhaps the hardest work on GLP-1 medications—knowing that and not letting the opportunity of that work pass you by. It's worth every bit of the journey to lean in and take the risk of loving yourself. That's not to say you can't have lots of help; you can. But there are no shortcuts to the work your soul asks you to do to remember it's safe to share its love in a world that repeatedly challenges that truth. It can be as simple as an aha moment, but I've found it's usually a mix of things: time, practice, conscious choosing, and vulnerability. And remember, your heart has all the tools to do this work; no amount of trauma takes away the capacity of your heart to do this work. Trauma causes a forgetfulness that your heart is capable, but it does not damage its ability to do the work of reclaiming/remembering your wholeness.

For instance, a student of mine blends Reiki, exercise, meditation, journaling, and therapy in her tool kit for healing her Inner Eater and emotional eating. All those modalities can help bring her to a place where synergy lines up. When coupled with her compassionate and peaceful attitude, she's ready to welcome home the parts she forgot or judges—the parts of her that think she is worthless and unlovable. But the modalities can't welcome her parts back into her heart for her; she must do that herself.

In other words, changing your belief system isn't something that happens with willpower, crystals, or eating anything you want. This work is about having the courage to welcome all your parts home, into the present, with unconditional love.

The Challenge to Love Ourselves

Remember a few chapters back when I mentioned that hard relationships with food and our body exist to challenge you to discover and transform untrue things you believe about yourself? Those untrue beliefs can manifest in a variety of ways: relationship problems, career struggles, even chronic illness. These issues often arise as a way to bring those beliefs to the surface, prompting us to examine and ultimately heal them.

Years of dieting, tears in dressing rooms, standing at the back of family photos, and snarky comments is how it starts. Then food becomes a way to cope to handle uncomfortable emotions that arose as a result. However, when we examine the root of these emotions, we often find that they're built upon false assumptions, such as "It was my fault," "If I try hard, I will be safe," or "I am no good, I was just made wrong." A self-compassionate lens reveals emotional eating as an opportunity—a guide, a map—to uncover these errors in our assumptions about our innate value and goodness. Through self-compassion and reparenting, we can see past the illusion of these perceived deficits, allowing us to live a more embodied life, grounded in our true worth and value.

Your journey on a GLP-1 and the peaks and valleys it has provided is a map into your heart, reminding you of your value and lovability. Because it's tenacious and involves food and body image, something we encounter daily, it serves as a constant reminder. While it may appear as a problem on the surface, a closer look reveals it as a blueprint to embrace our true selves as loving, wonderful people who have simply faced challenges that led us to believe otherwise.

The constant, lifelong battles with food and diets can take us out of the present moment, allowing us to avoid discomfort. In contrast, self-compassion brings us into the present moment with our heart and reminds us, "You can do this." Reparenting further reinforces this support with the message "I am with you."

Remember, beliefs can crystallize over time, and it takes effort and presence to break them down so we can access our innate love and share our true selves with the world. We tend to resist change, and emotional eating can both help us make sense of difficult change and hinder it by compensating for the discomfort it brings. However, the journey of GLP-1 can also increase our awareness of the crystallizations or compensations that hold us back from living the life we want. Now is the time to make the most of the opportunity that GLP-1 is giving you!

While our tendencies and patterns like emotional eating, chronic dieting, shopping, and bypassing conflict may seem to keep us from facing our challenges, they actually reveal our avoidance of discomfort. From a broader perspective, they show us that we are avoiding discomfort so we can choose a different, more loving option. Your GLP-1 is here to encourage you to choose the more loving option for yourself if you engage in the road map this book is laying out. In the past it may have seemed as though excessive food thoughts made you feel flawed, but it's crucial to remember that these thoughts are just thoughts, not reflections of your worth or character, which hopefully you have been able to experience on a GLP-1. Paradoxically, though, the more you allow all thoughts about food to surface without judgment, the less power they hold over you. But your ego will challenge this higher perspective and give you reasons to turn away from your pain and not trust your heart.

The universe wants you to learn and grow, and it will present you with challenges until you have nothing left to do but completely and wholly claim your innate goodness with radical authority. Imagine, for instance, that a part of you was so angry your husband cheated on you that you destroyed all his prized wooden flutes in a rage of grief and despair. I actually did that. I had to reconcile that I had it in me to do that—but not deem myself a bad person. I took responsibility for my actions by apologizing to my ex. Still, I also came to terms with the fact that I had it in me to be a destructive human who could seek revenge and feel a level of hopelessness I hadn't prior. I had to see that destructive part of me with the same love and compassion as the part that excelled at being a class parent for my daughter's kindergarten class.

When we try to elevate ourselves to be above things and be "spiritual" or "evolved" (an epidemic on social media right now), the universe will keep gifting us with challenges until we decide every part of us deserves our forgiveness, love, and connection. It isn't about being "above" challenges—*it's about loving ourselves in a challenge.* And because the universe works in mysterious ways, it created troubles with food and body image to keep us engaged in the challenge until we love ourselves so fully and completely that we don't care if we emotionally eat. Because we can't stop eating, it's the perfect setup to bring us closer to the parts of ourselves that we hate but that need us.

Remember, taking a GLP-1 medication, all the untrue things you believe about yourself will tuck themselves away and resurface through a different challenge and beckon you to choose trusting and loving yourself over self-persecution dressed up as a life drama. You don't want the lesson about your innate holiness to come through food? Okay, how about career or financial challenges? The soul's curriculum for the lessons you are here to understand doesn't get bypassed or erased. The universe loves you too much to forget about the wisdom-building you came here to do.

Our culture often defaults to self-criticism, as an attempt to heal, fall in line, and forge a path forward, especially around food, but this isn't our natural state. Our factory setting is living from our heart, expressing genuine kindness and support toward ourselves, even when in pain. Yet for those who lacked nurturing growing up, this can feel like being asked to do algebra without mastering fractions—unnatural and insurmountable.

How we see ourselves, our body, health, and food all become the manifestation of these unfelt emotions, stemming from untrue beliefs that drive us to undermine ourselves through food. It feels natural because, for some, it's all we've ever known.

The antidote to fear is remembering the love in our heart, our ultimate source of safety. Simply being willing to explore what it would feel like to make room for pain, rather than hide it, can initiate healing. This process doesn't involve bypassing or transcending pain, but rather consciously moving toward it with a kind heart and making space for it.

Dani's Story

In my practice, I often see unhealthy eating patterns develop from the stress of trying to make weight loss happen in a certain way, especially for those on GLP-1 medications. Dani, for instance, came to me after several months on her prescription. She had experienced an early burst of progress, but now her weight loss had stalled. This initially seemed like just a pause, but it quickly became a source of intense anxiety, fueled by the fear that this medication would be yet another letdown in her life. Dani had found support in online communities on Reddit and Facebook, where others shared similar journeys. At first, it felt like she had discovered a new group of people who understood her. But as she compared her own slow progress to their dramatic transformations, she began to feel left behind. The pressure became so intense that her days were filled with thoughts about what she might be doing wrong, scanning every detail for possible mistakes.

The fear of failing at this "last chance" for weight loss became overwhelming. Dani told me she felt terrified and distrustful of her own body. She believed that perfect eating and flawless medication adherence were her only defenses against regaining weight. The constant comparisons online amplified her sense of failure, leaving her anxious and exhausted. She wanted to push harder, restrict more, and control everything to prove she could succeed. She added extra gym sessions, lifted heavier weights, and increased her protein intake, convinced that if she could just get the formula right, the stall would break. While there is nothing wrong with making practical adjustments like ensuring adequate protein, these changes were fueled by an urgent need to fix herself. The harm was not in the actions themselves, but in the way she turned on herself when results did not come quickly. Harsh words and rigid expectations took root, planting false beliefs that she was failing, and those beliefs became the true obstacle—blocking her emotional growth.

Through our conversation, we explored the underlying emotions driving her desire for control: fear, shame, and discouragement. I encouraged Dani to check in with her Inner Eater, the part of her that wanted to take over and demand stricter rules. When she paused to ask this part what it was afraid of, the answer came quickly: it feared yet another failure. It believed that if she did not do everything perfectly, she would lose this opportunity and prove to herself that she could never succeed.

This realization helped Dani see that her Inner Eater's strictness was not cruelty, but protection. It was trying to shield her from disappointment. Self-compassion meant meeting herself exactly where she was, without judgment, and reparenting meant giving herself what she needed to feel safe. In her case, that was reassurance that she was not wrong, and this was not another example of life disappointing her.

With guidance, Dani accessed her compassionate heart space, offering warmth and understanding to her Inner Eater. This connection fostered a sense of shared responsibility, lessening the pressure. She began to see that she could feel the sting of disappointment without being disappointed in herself. The stall remained hard, but she no longer turned on herself in the process.

By communicating with her Inner Eater through compassion and curiosity, Dani forgave, understood, and integrated this part of herself. She shifted her focus from trying to control every detail of food and medication to relying on her inner resources for comfort and security. This transformation empowered her to navigate the uncertainty of her GLP-1 journey without falling back into restriction and self-persecution.

Dani's story illustrates how comparison, fear, and stalled progress can take over the weight loss journey. By meeting these challenges with self-compassion and practicing reparenting, we can hold space for our doubt, meet ourselves with safety, and continue forward without losing trust in who we are.

* * *

Challenges with food and your body is like a splinter in your big toe that you don't know is there. It's been around for so long that you've learned to live with it, judging yourself about how you walk a little lopsidedly. You know something is off, but you're not sure exactly what. On this journey with your splinter, you spend a lot of time developing amazing ways to compensate for it—special shoes, soft socks, pretty Band-Aids—and maybe you even define yourself as a "survivor of walking with a limp," instead of embracing radical vulnerability to discover and decide you are worth the special tool (your heart) to remove the splinter and live a more embodied life.

In this modern life, with the endless choices of how to "better" ourselves and prove to our egos (and the world) that we can self-improve enough to go on to become social media influencer stars, we forget that the journey of our heart is inward, ordinary, and available in each moment. Pulling a splinter out of your toe is ordinary, but it will change your life and help you walk better. And here is the universal gut-punch truth: Pulling out that splinter for the sake of striving for enlightenment, glory, and fame will call in another splinter—and another. Splinters will keep coming until you stop striving for enlightenment, glory, and fame and instead sit in the quiet miracle of welcoming yourself home to yourself over and over again... loving yourself as God/universe/source loves you.

Chapter Takeaways
- Many tools are available to us these days in the healing space, but some of them draw us outside of ourselves, away from the experience of our heart keeping us safe.
- Some messages in the healing space create a bypassing effect, so we can skirt pain or rise above it, but there are no substitutions for using our heart, which is the only thing that can truly help us.

- Ultimately, if we do bypass things, the universe often gives us another opportunity to deeply care for ourselves but in a different situation.
- Beyond the practical and pragmatic approaches of having a body and taking care of it, we will all face an event that challenges us to remember our innate goodness and use our heart as the tool to do that rather than food.
- We can all practice caring for and being loving to our hurt parts.

Chapter 12

The Maintenance Phase

One day at a time, and somehow one hour at a time, love will be enough to see us through, get us back on our feet and dust us off.
—Anne Lamott

Now I'll address the reality of post-medication life. Like most, your GLP-1 journey is likely to have many peaks and valleys. Peaks like finally feeling in control of your body and seeing the reversal of health markers. Maybe your blood pressure is finally in the normal range, and you've been able to taper off your medication. Valleys may include nausea, weight stalls, hair loss, or arguing with insurance companies over coverage. Whether you're tapering off medication completely or reducing your dosage, there may be changes in your body and thoughts during this phase, and it's best to expect and prepare for them. But, don't worry, you got this! You've made it this far, and you have plenty of exercises to help you navigate this new phase.

In this chapter, I'll explain why the skills you've been building throughout this book—working with your Inner Eater, understanding your Emotional Math, practicing the NICE protocol, and developing self-compassion through reparenting—become even more crucial during the maintenance phase. It's because these practices help you with any bumps or stressful uncertainty and form the foundation of sustainable healing that continues on.

The maintenance phase isn't about preventing all weight regain or eliminating all thoughts about food. Rather, it's about developing resilience while you navigate new territory and experiences. It's about leaning into a newly formed intuition based on your wholeness, not untrue beliefs. Let's navigate this transition with grace and self-compassion. Think of it as the next chapter in your healing journey, one where the skills you've been cultivating will truly shine.

Understanding the Post-Medication Landscape

When the effects of GLP-1 medications begin to diminish, many people experience specific fears and concerns. The most common worries I hear from clients include:

- "What if all the food noise comes rushing back?"
- "I'm terrified of regaining the weight I've lost."
- "The medication stopped working. Now what?"
- "Will I lose all the progress I've made?"
- "I don't trust myself to make good decisions without the medication."
- "I'm not sure who I am in this new body."

These fears are completely normal. As the effects of the medicine fade, you may notice more thoughts about food, increased hunger, and old emotional triggers around eating, food, and your body. Or you may be feeling as if you need a different playbook to navigate the new body you have.

No matter where you find yourself, what many see as "setbacks" are actually opportunities for deeper healing, and the maintenance phase is all about putting what you've learned in the book into practice. Really remember that! All the new practices you've been learning are like a new language. When you first learn a new language, you just speak a few sentences, but as you practice a new language, you will start to feel more and more confident. So, think of maintenance as the time to do this. Keep this book handy. Read and reread passages and chapters. Practice connecting with your Inner Eater when you feel totally fine, not just when you feel dysregulated. Remember, the medication may have provided valuable space and time to develop new skills, but the real transformation occurs when you can apply these skills during challenging moments.

The biological and psychological components at play during this transition are complex. Your body is adjusting to new hormonal levels, your brain's reward pathways are recalibrating, and your emotional connection to food is shifting. Understanding these changes as natural rather than personal failures is the first step toward navigating them successfully.

Applying the NICE Protocol in the Maintenance Phase

The NICE protocol (Notice-Include-Comfort-Experience) becomes particularly powerful during the maintenance phase, when anxiety about food and body may intensify. Let's look at how each component specifically addresses the challenges of this transition:

Notice: During maintenance, you may notice an increase in food-related thoughts or judgments about your body. The practice of simply noticing these thoughts—"I'm having the thought that I'll lose control without the medication" or "I notice I'm feeling anxious about being hungrier today"—creates crucial space between you and these thoughts. This space allows you to respond thoughtfully rather than react automatically.

Include: Rather than fighting against renewed hunger or food thoughts, the practice of inclusion acknowledges them as part of your experience without judgment. This might sound like: "I'm including my fear about weight regain as part of my experience right now. It's here with me, and that's okay."

Comfort: Self-comfort becomes especially important when navigating the emotional turbulence of the maintenance phase. Offering yourself genuine compassion might sound like: "Of course I'm feeling uncertain right now—my body is going through another transition. This is hard, and I'm doing my best."

Experience: Fully experiencing the physical and emotional sensations of this transition—without trying to fix or change them—builds resilience. Notice how your body feels as hunger returns, how emotions arise and pass, and how you can be present with all of it.

Daily practice of the NICE protocol during maintenance helps normalize the experience and reduces panic or anxiety about normal physical and emotional changes. For example, one client used the protocol when she noticed heightened anxiety before meals after reducing her medication. She shared, "I notice I'm feeling anxious about eating lunch today. I'm including this anxiety as part of my experience without trying to push it away. I'm offering myself comfort—this transition is challenging, and it makes sense I'm feeling uncertain. Now I'm experiencing the sensations in my body as I stay with these feelings." This practice, repeated daily, helped her move through the maintenance phase with greater ease and self-understanding.

Reconnecting with Your Inner Eater After Medication

One of the most significant effects of GLP-1 medications is how they can temporarily quiet your Inner Eater, that part of you that has complex feelings, beliefs, and needs related to food. As medication effects diminish, your Inner Eater may become more vocal, which can feel alarming if you're not prepared. If that happens, it will be okay. You have been building tools for this.

Rather than seeing this as a problem, consider it an opportunity to deepen your relationship with this important part of yourself. Your Inner Eater may have been less active during medication, but it has always been there, and now it needs your attention and care. It needs to know you are there for it and may want you to show it that it's not alone, or it hasn't done anything wrong. Expect this. Prepare for this—it's part of the journey.

Try this five-step dialogue technique specifically designed for the maintenance phase:

1. In a quiet space where you won't be disturbed, take a few centering breaths.
2. Begin by acknowledging your Inner Eater: "I know you've been quieter while I've been on medication, and now you may have more to say. I'm here to listen."
3. Ask gentle questions: "What are you afraid might happen during this transition? What do you need from me right now? How can I make you feel safe as things change?"
4. Listen without judgment to whatever arises—feelings of fear, anger, vulnerability, or confusion are all welcome.
5. Offer reassurance: "We're in this together. I won't abandon you, even as things change."

Remember that your Inner Eater may have legitimate concerns about the transition that deserve attention. Perhaps it fears a return to painful food restriction or worries about losing the physical gains that came with medication. By creating space for these concerns and meeting them with compassion, you build safety within rather than relying on external controls. The path you've been building has been about inner resilience—confidence that you can support yourself as you experience the transition of maintenance rather than external validation.

One of my clients discovered her Inner Eater was terrified of being "controlled" again, after experiencing the freedom that came with reduced food thoughts while on medication. By acknowledging this fear and promising to maintain an attitude of curiosity rather than control, she helped her Inner Eater feel secure during the transition. Remember it's about cooperation rather than acceptance. Maintenance is truly the zone of cooperation!

Beyond Emotional Math: Finding Deeper Balance
As the effects of GLP-1 medications change, you may notice shifts in your emotional math calculations around food. The medication may have temporarily simplified these calculations by reducing hunger and cravings, making decisions about food feel easier. As these effects fade, the complex emotional math may return—perhaps even intensified by fear of losing progress.

This is when the deeper work begins. Rather than getting caught in the numbers and judgments of emotional math, you can focus on the parts of yourself engaged in these calculations:
- The part that fears returning to old patterns
- The part that equates food choices with moral value
- The part that believes control equals safety
- The part that worries about others' judgments

Each of these parts needs compassionate attention. For example, when you notice yourself calculating whether you "should" eat something, pause and ask: "Which part of me is doing this calculation? What is it trying to protect me from?" You can imagine these thoughts as clouds or text bubbles that are temporary and not all-consuming like they previously have been.

Creating new mental frameworks that honor both physical and emotional needs becomes crucial during maintenance. This may mean distinguishing between physical hunger (which can increase as medication effects fade) and emotional hunger (which might intensify due to anxiety about the transition).

Practical strategies for when emotional math becomes overwhelming again include:

- Pausing to identify which part of you is speaking
- Using the NICE protocol with the specific calculations
- Asking "What do I need right now?" rather than "What should I eat/not eat?"
- Remembering that food choices are not moral decisions

One client developed a simple mantra that helped her when emotional math intensified: "This calculation is trying to keep me safe. I can acknowledge it and still make choices based on what I truly need."

Self-Compassion as Your Foundation

During the maintenance phase, self-compassion becomes more crucial than ever. The physiological changes occurring as medication effects diminish can trigger shame, self-criticism, and fear, exactly when you need kindness the most. This phase is when you pull the new tool of self-compassion out of your pocket and use it when or if you feel old patterns creeping back. Offer those patterns a place at the table with you. As you touch old patterns with your compassionate care, they transform from old ghosts haunting you to allies that form a new army of emotional resilience.

Self-compassion isn't just a nice idea during this phase; it's the foundation that makes all other practices possible. It says "You will never be alone, and I will always be with you." Those are the words that many of us never heard growing up and caused us to believe untrue things about ourselves. In an odd way maintenance is asking you to spread your own love even deeper and further, which will help prevent any increased hunger or food thoughts from spiraling into shame and self-judgment. Your heart was built to do this. All the tools are ready for you to implement. No matter what you have previously experienced or believed about yourself, self-compassion only needs practice (read: you have to vote for yourself). Just step on the gas because you were born with the engine—you may have just forgotten that truth.

When working with potential weight changes during maintenance, self-compassion practices may include:

- Acknowledging the difficulty of the situation: "This transition is challenging, and it makes sense that I'm struggling."
- Recognizing common humanity: "Many people find this phase difficult—I'm not alone in this experience."

- Offering kindness rather than criticism: "I'm doing my best to navigate complex changes. I deserve patience during this process."

Meeting yourself with kindness during physiological transitions means honoring your body's signals, which may include increased hunger. Rather than fighting against them, it's the time to recognize that your worth isn't determined by your body size or food choices. This is easier to do when you come from a place of understanding and believing that you can trust your transition. Trusting transition can be especially hard for those who have had a history of trauma. The old thought may have been: "Everyone I care about lets me down. I will always be alone." Self-compassion is the bridge you can trust here to change that narrative. "In the past, transitions have been terrifying because no one was there to help me through them. Now I will be the one to do this rather than depending on others. In fact, I'm the best person to do this."

Remember that self-compassion builds resilience by creating an internal environment where mistakes and struggles aren't catastrophes but opportunities for learning and growth. This resilience is exactly what you need to navigate the inevitable challenges of the maintenance phase.

Vanessa's Journey Through Maintenance

My client Vanessa illustrates how we weave in and out of old patterns like emotional eating, particularly when medication enters the equation. Let's examine her journey and see how she applied the principles we've discussed to navigate the challenges of the maintenance phase.

Vanessa grew up never feeling good in her body and believed she'd never be good enough. She couldn't remember a time when she didn't feel self-conscious. Her mom was a chronic dieter who also never felt good enough, so Vanessa was surrounded by the message that having a smaller body was better. She was also bullied for her body size throughout her childhood. Attending school was incredibly challenging for her because of this, and she struggled to make close friends. She felt shame about her body and how she looked. As a result, she internalized the message "I'll never be good enough." Vanessa felt that if she could just change her body and mold it into a shape that would get praise from others, including her mother, she would be likable, good enough, and would feel better about herself. After leaving home as a young adult, she explored intuitive eating and anti-diet culture to find refuge from the constant war she was in with her natural body size. This helped her accept herself and find peace she hadn't yet found.

Below, I break down the timeline of how Vanessa's journey unfolded, including her experience with GLP-1 medication and the emotional work that accompanied it.

Pre-Medication Journey

Vanessa moved through various phases, from being immersed in diet culture to exploring anti-diet approaches like intuitive eating. Each step brought her closer to understanding her relationship with food and her body, but the core beliefs about her worthlessness remained unaddressed. She wavered in and out of several styles of eating, never calling them "diets," and still secretly wished her body was different, but she learned to find a more middle path than growing up.

Personal Crisis and Medical Intervention

After being married for a decade, Vanessa and her husband separated. This was a big challenge, and she found navigating single motherhood and co-parenting extremely stressful, so she "stress ate." She gained fifty pounds, and her doctor recommended trying a GLP-1 medication to address some metabolic health concerns that had developed from her recent weight gain. Initially, Vanessa resisted, seeing it as "giving in" to diet culture, but eventually she decided to try it as a health intervention rather than a weight-loss solution.

Medication Experience and Self-Discovery

The GLP-1 medication helped regulate Vanessa's appetite and cravings, which initially felt like relief but later created confusion about her body signals. Was her reduced hunger "real" or medication-induced? Through working with me, she began practicing self-compassion for this confusion. She allowed herself to be curious and experiment without feeling "wrong." Together, we discovered that she never worked on the core belief that she was worthless, which formed after being bullied in school and watching her mother chronically diet from disliking her own body. We made a plan to address that belief, rather than focusing solely on body neutrality or medication effects.

During this stage, Vanessa began using the NICE protocol daily. She would *notice* her thoughts about food and weight, *include* them in her awareness without judgment, *comfort* herself for having these perfectly normal responses and forgive herself for feeling worthless, and fully *experience* the sensations and emotions that arose. This practice helped her create space between herself and her thoughts, allowing her to respond more thoughtfully.

Vanessa also began working with her Inner Eater, who she discovered was terrified of rejection. Through gentle dialogues, she learned that her Inner Eater used food to soothe the pain of feeling worthless and unwanted. As the medication reduced her physical hunger, she had more emotional capacity to attend to these deeper needs of her Inner Eater.

Integration and Deeper Understanding

Vanessa recognized that many of her body liberation views were built upon trying to stay safe, rather than addressing the untrue beliefs she held about herself. As the medication helped create space between her and her food cravings, she could see more clearly how she had used food to soothe emotional pain. She also began to question her relationship with the medication: Was it a temporary tool or something she needed long-term? This questioning led to deeper self-exploration.

As Vanessa prepared for the maintenance phase, she deepened her practice of the NICE protocol, particularly focusing on noticing and including fears about what would happen when the medication effects diminished. She practiced comforting the parts of herself that were afraid of "losing control" and fully experiencing the physical sensations of these fears without judgment.

Her work with her Inner Eater became more profound as she prepared for maintenance. She asked her Inner Eater what it needed to feel safe as the medication effects changed and was surprised to discover it wasn't asking for unlimited food but rather reassurance that Vanessa wouldn't abandon it when things got hard.

Creating a Sustainable Path

Vanessa stayed focused on kindness toward herself, regardless of how she decided to eat, whether she continued medication, or what size she was. She developed a plan for eventually transitioning off the GLP-1 medication, incorporating both the physical aspects (gradual dosage reduction) and emotional preparation (developing alternative coping strategies). Every day, she practiced self-soothing, self-kindness, and working with the parts of herself that emerged as she navigated how to best care for her body—no matter what that care looked like.

During the maintenance phase itself, Vanessa faced several challenges. When her hunger increased after reducing her medication dosage, she found herself initially panicking. She used the NICE protocol to create space: "I notice I'm feeling afraid about being hungrier today. I'm including this fear as part of my experience. I'm comforting myself because this transition is naturally challenging. I'm experiencing the sensations of hunger without judgment."

She continued dialoguing with her Inner Eater, who needed extra reassurance during this transition. She would set aside time each morning to check in: "What do you need today? How can I help you feel safe as things change?" Sometimes the answer was surprising—her Inner Eater often needed emotional connection or creative expression more than it needed food.

The emotional math calculations around food became more complex during maintenance, but Vanessa had developed skills to navigate them. When she found herself in spiral of calculations about "should" and "shouldn't," she would pause and identify which part of herself was speaking. Often, it was the part that believed her worth was tied to her size—a belief she could now recognize and respond to with compassion.

You can see that Vanessa's viewpoint evolved over time. Life's challenges helped her widen her perspective and understand that there is no final destination point—just a willingness to experiment to see what would work for her. The GLP-1 medication became neither hero nor villain in her story but simply one tool among many that helped her create space to address deeper emotional needs. Over time, she let go of the right/wrong viewpoint and instead began trusting herself and her choices—even if they changed over time, even if they included what some would consider a "diet" or medication.

Creating Your Personalized Maintenance Plan

The maintenance phase looks different for everyone, which is why creating a personalized plan is so important. This section will guide you through developing a strategy that honors your unique needs, challenges, and goals during this transition.

Begin by identifying your personal maintenance triggers and vulnerabilities:

- **Physical triggers**: How does your body respond to medication reduction? Do you notice increased hunger, cravings, or energy fluctuations?
- **Emotional triggers**: Which emotions are most challenging for you when it comes to food? Anxiety, loneliness, boredom, anger, or stress?
- **Situational triggers**: Are there specific situations (social events, work stress, family dynamics) that challenge your relationship with food?
- **Belief triggers**: Which core beliefs about yourself tend to activate when food and body issues arise?

Once you've identified these triggers, you can build a customized toolkit, drawing from all the practices we've explored:

- **For physical triggers**: Specific NICE protocol practices that help you respond to physical sensations with awareness and compassion.
- **For emotional triggers**: Inner Eater dialogues that address the specific emotions that challenge you most.
- **For situational triggers**: Preparation strategies for challenging situations, including self-compassion practices before, during, and after these events.
- **For belief triggers**: Reparenting practices like Placing the Loving that specifically address your core untrue beliefs.

Remember that your needs will change throughout the maintenance phase, so your plan should include strategies for adapting your practices. For example, you might need more frequent Inner Eater dialogues or Placing the Loving exercises during the initial reduction of medication, and more focus on emotional math as your hunger signals return.

Working with healthcare providers during this transition is crucial. Discuss your psychological preparation alongside the physical aspects of medication reduction. Some providers may not be familiar with the emotional challenges of this phase, so be prepared to advocate for support with both the physical and emotional components of maintenance.

When Things Get Hard: Returning to Core Practices
Even with the best preparation, challenging periods during maintenance are normal and expected. Learning to recognize when you need additional support and how to provide it for yourself is key to long-term success. Signs that you may need to deepen your practice include:
- Increased frequency or intensity of food preoccupation
- Return of harsh self-judgment or rigid rules around eating
- Feeling disconnected from your body's signals
- Using food to cope with emotions more frequently
- Anxiety or panic about weight changes

When you notice these signs, return to the following five core practices we've explored, but with increased frequency and intensity:

1. **Daily NICE protocol practice:** Set aside specific times each day to practice, perhaps morning and evening, plus brief check-ins throughout the day.
2. **Regular Inner Eater dialogues:** Schedule regular times to connect with this part of yourself. Give yourself five extra minutes to do this—in the car, before you get out of bed, or while you are folding laundry.
3. **Placing the Loving:** Practice when you have 10-15 minutes or when you have painful memories surface.
4. **Written self-compassion exercises:** Journal letters to yourself from the perspective of unconditional love and acceptance as you are in maintenance.
5. **Body-centered practices:** Gentle movement like yoga or walking, conscious breathing, or a simple breath before eating will help you stay connected to your physical experience.

Remember that maintenance is not a linear process. Periods of challenge and ease will naturally cycle, and needing to intensify your practice isn't a sign of failure—it's a sign of awareness and self-care. Permission to adjust your approach based on what you discover is essential during maintenance. What worked during the medication phase may need modification now, and what works during one stage of maintenance may change as your body and mind continue to adapt.

Practice: Maintenance Meditation and Journaling Prompts
Below is a guided meditation and journaling exercise specifically designed

for the maintenance phase. These practices will help you process the complex feelings that arise during this transition and strengthen your connection with your Inner Eater.

Maintenance Phase Meditation
Find a comfortable position where you can be both alert and relaxed. Allow your eyes to close or keep them softly focused.

Begin by bringing awareness to your breath, noticing the natural rhythm without trying to change it. With each inhale, imagine gathering compassion and understanding. With each exhale, release judgment and criticism.

Now, bring awareness to your body. Notice any sensations present today—hunger, fullness, tension, or calm. Whatever you discover, simply acknowledge it with kindness. Your body is going through a transition, and all sensations are information, not problems to solve.

Imagine your Inner Eater sitting across from you. How does this part of you appear today? What expression is on its face? What might it want to tell you about this transition period?

Listen with openness and curiosity. This part of you has weathered many changes like diets, lifestyle shifts, and medication effects, and it holds wisdom about both your needs and fears. Ask your Inner Eater: "What do you need from me during this maintenance phase? How can I help you feel safe as things change?" Listen deeply to the response, without judgment or correction.

Now, imagine extending warmth and reassurance to your Inner Eater. Perhaps you see yourself sitting beside it, offering comfort through your presence. Perhaps you imagine a gentle light of compassion surrounding both of you.

Remind your Inner Eater: "We're in this together. I won't abandon you when things get challenging. I'm committed to understanding what you need and responding with kindness."

Take a few more breaths, feeling the connection between you and your Inner Eater strengthening. When you're ready, slowly bring your awareness back to the room, opening your eyes if they were closed.

Maintenance Phase Journaling Prompts
Use the following prompts to deepen your understanding of your needs during the maintenance phase. I recommend setting aside time weekly

to reflect on these questions, perhaps creating a regular check-in ritual that helps you monitor your emotional well-being during this transition. Remember that the maintenance phase is not just about maintaining physical changes; it's about maintaining and deepening the relationship with yourself that you've been building all along. It's about trusting the tool kit is there, and you only need to call upon it. Your heart is prepared to do this work!

- What fears arise when I think about reduced medication effects? What is the story beneath these fears?
- When I notice increased hunger, what thoughts and judgments appear? How can I apply the NICE protocol to these experiences?
- What does my Inner Eater need most during this transition? How can I provide this, either through food or through other forms of nourishment?
- What forms of emotional math have become more active during maintenance? Which parts of me are performing these calculations, and what do they need?
- How has my definition of "success" evolved throughout this journey? What would true success look like during the maintenance phase?
- What would I say to a dear friend going through this exact same transition? How can I offer myself the same kindness?
- What challenges have I already navigated successfully in my relationship with food? What strengths did I discover through those experiences?
- How can I honor both my physical and emotional needs during this transition?

* * *

The skills you've learned like working with your Inner Eater, practicing the NICE protocol, Placing the Loving, understanding emotional math, and cultivating self-compassion will provide everything you need to navigate this phase and not feel alone or abandoned. It's truly the time to go deeper, even if you feel nervous or scared. This is the time to *lean in* and put everything you've learned into practice, and remember that you will never be alone because your heart will keep you company. Maintenance isn't about perfection; it's about meeting yourself where you are without judgement.

Putting It All into Practice

Here we are at the end of this book and at the beginning of you implementing a new framework of living your life. I'm so excited for you that I feel like I'm going to burst! You probably have thought so often during your GLP-1 journey about what the future from here on out will look like. My hope and prayer for you is that it will be better than you can imagine. You have all the tools, and now it's time to fly to new lands. It's time for you believe in yourself and start sharing your gifts, because no one on this planet possesses the same unique kind of love that you hold in your heart.

For so many of us, the journey to get here has been hard won. With a small shift in perspective, you can bring to light the incorrect data you have based your worthiness on, and you can change it right now through the power of your heart.

As this book laid out, you can easily learn the skills to deepen your trust in yourself, and that will have far-reaching positive consequences for your health, body, and relationship with food. Food noise may return and you might still emotionally eat, and that's okay; the point is not forgetting your loving self when hard things like that do happen. This book is helping you to rewrite your emotional resilience setpoint, so you have real skills to support yourself no matter what the future holds, and being hard on yourself will be optional, not essential like before. Emotional eating helps you understand something about yourself for your benefit. Your heart is prepared to do the heavy lifting for you in life when you are challenged next.

I urge you to embrace your student mind as you journey into your heart. Everything is here to help you remember that you can trust the power of your heart to keep you safe above all else. Your inner goodness will remain wholly intact no matter what happens to you, and all the trials and tribulations in life are opportunities reminding you that you can lean in and trust.

You have inside of you the tools to do this work—assisted by the exercises in this book—to practice opening the treasure you were born with. As you begin, it may seem unnatural, unintuitive, and awkward, but I promise it will provide the treasure you seek. Taking the time to learn and practice holding uncomfortable feelings, often based on false assumptions about yourself, will improve your relationship with food and your body more than you thought imaginable.

While there is no substitute for practice, I know you can do this. You now have the blueprint to go inward and discover the power of your heart, trust your life, and lovingly reclaim your hurt parts—but you will have to take the journey and experience it to know it's true. I know this: The universe is built on unconditional loving, and voting for yourself ushers in unconditional love for the journey you are taking. You are deeply supported, even if you can't see it right now, and I will be cheering you on as well.

The exercises in this book are meant to support you in moving away from the false outward safety that you may have built up over the years, questioning yourself and how you were made, and seeing yourself. Today that changes, and you step forward into a new place where supporting yourself comes before judging yourself. To do that, I encourage you to consider what parts of yourself you haven't yet invited into your heart because they seem too risky. Bringing those parts back into yourself will naturally reduce the tendency to search for safety outside yourself through habits like firing up a harsh critical voice. The main ingredients you need to set up the inner scene to reparent and love yourself are your imagination, visualization, practice, and intention—and all are available inside of you right now.

Remember, doing this work reprograms the bad data, or corrupted file your inner computer has been running one loving thought at a time. Disliking your body, struggling with how to have peaceful relationship with food, like all struggles, provides an opportunity for each of us, prompting a practical and personal journey. Practically speaking, recognizing this means taking the step to look at what you believe and where you hold pain and trusting that you can care for yourself. But it also means you are allowed full freedom to care for yourself without fear of labels.

You don't have to identify with body positivity, body neutrality, intuitive eating, anti-diet, body liberation, or any other concept. Loving yourself is bigger than any label, movement, or philosophy, and it's cultivated inside of you with one phrase: "Did I learn to be loving?" Holding that alive inside yourself, for yourself, will guide you to the place where your warm, healing love has been cut out, shut off, or deemed too risky.

My hope is that today is the day you vote for yourself, because the world needs your loving in it, and all the challenges that come along with having a body are disguised to help you do this. Making room for and staying curious about the part of you that is struggling with where your GLP-1 journey will take you is just the start. You got this. The safety you seek is alive in your heart right now, and it will never run out. I love you.

Notes

Acknowledgements

I want to express my deepest gratitude to my family for their unwavering support throughout the journey to write this book. To my husband, Derek, who saw the vision for this book and spent hours helping me make it a reality. To my best friends, Trisha, Laurie, and Cynthia, who spent hours talking on the phone, taking walks with me, and helping me flush out ideas that proved instrumental in writing this book and helping me clarify my message. Thank you so much for the support and unconditional love. To my identical twin sister, Danielle, who not only supported me but walked the path of compassion as we found our soul family, together.

A special thanks to my literary agent, Joelle Delbourgo, for believing in this idea and guiding me so calmly through the publishing process.

To my editors, Lara Asher, who helped me give form to my ideas again and again, served as a loving sounding board and was a fantastic cheerleader; and Shannon Littrell, who helped shape the manuscript into a cohesive whole.

Heartfelt thanks to my clients and students who risked it all to vote for themselves and discover the power of their hearts to heal. Thank you for trusting me to witness your process.

Finally, to my teachers, Dr. Robert Waterman and Karey Thorne, who created and held the sacred space for me to remember myself, and my worthiness, and to discover the power of my heart.

About the Author

Jessica Brown is a Stanford-certified compassion teacher, functional medicine clinical nutritionist, and author with over 25 years of experience helping people heal physically and emotionally. With more than ten years of specialized clinical practice in self-compassion-based reparenting and mindset work, she has guided thousands toward lasting transformation.

Jessica is the author of "The Loving Diet," which pioneered mind-body approaches for autoimmune conditions, and served as visiting faculty at the Institute of Integrative Nutrition, where she helped create their Mindful Eating program. She maintains a thriving practice as a consultant to practitioners nationwide and continues to influence the health community through her innovative approaches to healing.

Her work bridges the gap between medical treatment and emotional healing, offering practical tools for those ready to transform their relationship with food, body, and self from the inside out. Jessica lives with her family in Marin County, CA.

You can find her at www.thelovingdiet.com